# MAGAZINE-MADE AMERICA

## THE CULTURAL TRANSFORMATION OF THE POSTWAR PERIODICAL

# THE HAMPTON PRESS COMMUNICATION SERIES

## Mass Communications and Journalism
Lee Becker, supervisory editor

Magazine-Made America: The Cultural Transformation of the Postwar Periodical
*David Abrahamson*

American Heroes in the Media Age
*Susan J. Drucker and Robert S. Cathcart (eds.)*

Media, Sex and the Adolescent
*Bradley S. Greenberg, Jane D. Brown and Nancy Buerkel-Rothfuss*

*forthcoming*

Growing Up with Popular Music
*Peter G. Christenson and Donald F. Roberts*

Newspapers and Social Change: Community Structure and Coverage of Critical Events
*John C. Pollock*

# MAGAZINE-MADE AMERICA

## THE CULTURAL TRANSFORMATION OF THE POSTWAR PERIODICAL

### DAVID ABRAHAMSON
*NORTHWESTERN UNIVERSITY*

 HAMPTON PRESS, INC.
CRESSKILL, NEW JERSEY

Printed in the United States of America

**Library of Congress Cataloging-in-Publication Data**

Abrahamson, David.
    Magazine-made America : the cultural transformation of the postwar
periodical / David Abrahamson
        p.   cm. -- (The Hampton Press communication series)
    Includes bibliographical references and indexes
    ISBN: 1-57273-008-0. -- ISBN 1-57273-009-9 (pbk.)
    1. American periodicals--History--20th century.  2. Journalism--
Social aspects--United States.  3. Pressure groups--United States--
Periodicals.  I. Title.  II. Series.
PN4877.A27    1996
051'.09'045--dc20                                        96-4402
                                                           CIP

Hampton Press, Inc.
23 Broadway
Cresskill, NJ 07626

For Barbara

# CONTENTS

# ACKNOWLEDGMENTS

This effort certainly could not have been completed without the generous guidance of my former colleagues at New York University. In particular, grateful acknowledgment is offered to Paul R. Baker, special mentor and even more special friend, as well as Richard Cunningham, Michael Norman, Neil Postman, and David M. Reimers. For their interest and suggestions, thanks are also due Aaron Feinsot, James Jasper, Janatha Pollock, Carl Prince, Jay Rosen, Mitchell Stephens, and Martin S. Walker.

A number of prominent executives were kind enough to share both advice and professional recollections. For their assistance, I would like to thank Paul Chook, P. Robert Farley, Bernard Finger, Stanley R. Greenfield, J. Michael Hadley, Furman Hebb, William Jeanes, Philip Korsant, Archa Knowlton, Donald D. Kummerfeld, the late Thomas Mandel, Leon Mandel, Gilbert C. Maurer, John O'Toole, James Manousos, William Phillips, Herbert Stern, Steven L. Thompson, and William Ziff. Their insights made an important contribution both to my understanding and to the historical record.

And for their kindness and encouragement in ways large and small, I would like to express my gratitude to Michael Janeway, Abe Peck, and Pat Clinton, my colleagues here at Northwestern University's Medill School of Journalism.

# 1

# INTRODUCTION

THE AMERICAN WAS DEVOTED TO PRACTICAL LABOR BUT FOND
OF MATERIAL COMFORT, JEALOUS OF HIS PRIVATE INDEPEN-
DENCE BUT EAGER FOR PUBLIC APPROVAL OF OTHERS.
      —JACKSON LEARS (1989, P. 51)

Late one Monday in the fall of 1960 two men nodded stiff greetings to each other in an overheated Chicago television studio. Then, as over 70 million Americans watched, Vice President Richard M. Nixon and Senator John F. Kennedy began the first presidential campaign debate of the Television Age. Although the occasion's printed text suggested the debate was a draw, in "image" terms, Kennedy clearly prevailed. With its inherent primacy of image over argument, the power of television to reach and sway mass audiences would soon be apparent. Perhaps even before the studio lights cooled, Nixon's front-running lead had begun to evaporate, Kennedy's prospects had brightened, and American politics had been changed forever.[1]

1

In retrospect, national electoral politics may not have been the only aspect of popular culture transformed by television's ascendant role that September 26 evening in 1960. And it is perhaps fitting that two of the reigning national media institutions that would ultimately be most dramatically affected, the mass-circulation magazines *Life* and *Look*, took surprisingly little notice of the event. The cover of the next week's *Life*, for example, featured Doris Day, and a small weekly news roundup item on the television debate was overpowered by a major pictorial essay entitled "Lovely Aspirants for the Role of First Lady: With Wifely Charm Pat Nixon and Jackie Kennedy Keep the Home Fires Burning." Even the closest readers of *Look*'s next issue would find no mention of the televised confrontation at all, but few could have missed the magazine's lavishly illustrated feature on "The Kennedy Women."[2] Within a year, however, television would become Americans' primary source of information about the world, and, as a result, by the end of the decade the character and structure of the U.S. magazine publishing industry would be forcibly transformed.

Most important, the commercial implications of television's pivotal role in the 1960 election were not lost on the marketing decision makers at America's large consumer-goods corporations and their advertising agencies. What television could do for a national political candidate, it might also accomplish for other mass-market products. For the prevailing consumer magazine form, the large circulation mass-audience publication, the economic implications were soon as disquieting as they were unavoidable. Siphoning away national advertising revenues, television quickly became the arch enemy.[3] Indeed, by the early 1970s three of the once dominant general-interest titles, *Life*, *Look*, and the *Saturday Evening Post*, having lost to television significant portions of both their national advertising incomes and their audiences' loyalty, were all forced to cease publication.[4]

In their place, another genre of magazine, the "special-interest" publication, began to flourish. Edited for specific, smaller audiences, addressing particular reader interests related to specific leisure activities, special-interest magazines with titles as diverse as the nation's newfound avocational pursuits (*Boating, Car and Driver, Cycle, Flying, Golf, Popular Electronics, Popular Photography, Skiing, Stereo Review, Tennis*, etc.) blossomed during the 1960s. In retrospect, it can be argued that they had two distinct advantages: Unlike their general-audience brethren, they were not in competition with television for mass-market advertising dollars; and perhaps more importantly, the nature and specificity of their subjects enjoyed a unique resonance with the underlying temper of the times.

## THE ARGUMENT

In his grand survey of popular culture, *The Unembarrassed Muse*, Russel Nye (1970, p. 4) argues that "popular art has been an unusually sensitive and accurate reflector of the attitudes and concerns of the society for which it is produced." More specifically, contemporary communication theorists such as John Pauly of St. Louis University suggest that all of the popular media in America represent "shared systems of meaning [allowing both] senders and receivers [to] compete and collaborate in constructing reality" (Pauly, 1991, pp. 2-3; see also Carey, 1989; Postman, 1985, 1988). As a result, all communication media have an important societal dimension, both reflecting and shaping the social actualities of their time. Though some scholars have called for more empirical research to support this argument, and critics have rightly noted the somewhat suspicious popularity of the "mirror metaphor" with media chieftains, this work will attempt to advance the argument that the emergence of the special-interest magazine in the 1960s was both a product of and contributor to major sociocultural and economic changes in postwar America.[5]

The origin of these changes was the unprecedented economic expansion following World War II. The resulting increases in affluence, education, and leisure time all contributed to a major transformation of society in the decade and a half after the war. Some observers believed that for the first time in any nation's history, a large majority of citizens was becoming economically enfranchised, and that the cornucopia of consumer goods might produce a classless society. Enveloped in the broad social consensus of the 1950s, many Americans had indeed, in David Potter's words, become "a people of plenty."[6]

With the arrival of the 1960s, however, although the plenitude continued, the social consensus did not. The discontinuities of that decade have, of course, been well documented, typically in terms of the widespread protest—often idealistic and, in its early manifestations, reformist—against the prevailing social and political norms. But there is also evidence to suggest that America underwent a concurrent, perhaps even broader based, social change of some significance in the early 1960s. Less concerned with contemporary aspirations for political and social justice, the social transformation was driven instead by a desire on the part of many for personal fulfillment and defined by new notions of identity and individualism, class and community, and leisure consumption and competence. For many Americans, the social coherence and unity of the 1950s gave way to what has been termed a "cult of domestic privatism." According to the social historian Loren Baritz, "Personality . . . [became] the decisive private property of the American middle class . . . nurtured and fondled as avidly as Midas caressed his gold" (Baritz, 1980, p. 313).[7]

This shift in the dominant value set, well before both the individualism reported by Tom Wolfe that so characterized the "Me Decade" of the 1970s (Wolfe, 1976, pp. 25-32) and the acquisitiveness of the 1980s (the "Gimme Decade"), might be called "The Other 1960s." It both provided the societal context from which modern special-interest magazines arose and was significantly furthered by their success.

## THE LITERATURE

As a generalization about journalism scholarship, magazines have drawn less attention as a research subject than either newspapers or television. A study conducted in the mid-1980s covering 20 years of issues of the profession's research journal, *Journalism Quarterly*, found that magazine subjects represented only 6% of the articles, and more than half of them were somewhat narrowly focused on journalistic "content analyses."[8] A similar survey of *Communication Abstracts* found that scholarly articles about magazines account for less than 1% of the contents; in comparison, research concerning newspapers represent more than 5% of the articles, and television, more than 20%.[9]

Part of the reason for this might be that, even though magazines are a popular major in many university journalism and mass communication departments, instruction in magazine research is part of the curriculum at only a small number of institutions. A larger systemic issue, however, is also a possibility. "Much magazine study has been limited to discussion of magazine publishing as a branch of the craft of journalism, or to analysis of the content of particular magazines because of some editorial or authorial prominence," wrote Dorothy Schmidt, a cultural historian. "Academic disciplines have almost routinely concentrated on the other legs of the print triad [i.e., newspapers and books] . . . but scant attention is given to the continuing role of magazines as reflectors and molders of public opinion and political and social attitudes (Schmidt, 1989, pp. 648-649).

Most historical scholarship related to American magazines, moreover, can be characterized as "chronicle," for much of it includes neither broad historical interpretation of the sociocultural contexts nor detailed insights into the defining economic realities of the medium. The principal reason for this is that in most instances media scholars have chosen to study magazines as isolated journalistic artifacts, rather than as products and catalysts of social, cultural, and economic change. Though often commendable as examples of archival rigor, the results have rarely been able to place magazines within their larger social frame. Clearly, this is the case regarding the major expansion of the special-interest magazine genre shortly after 1960.[10]

In the last 20 years, nevertheless, a few media scholars have proposed descriptive models to account for the trend toward increasing specialization in magazines. Three of the more interesting have been advanced by Richard Maisel, a New York University sociologist; Louisiana State University's John Merrill and the University of Florida's Ralph Lowenstein, both journalism scholars; and Antoon van Zuilen, a journalism historian at the University of Amsterdam. In summary form, the essential structure of each can be outlined as follows:

Maisel's three-stage model of social change and media growth builds on the established two-stage model of media development, first elaborated by Harold Innis, an economic historian, which suggests a functional relationship between a society's preindustrial-to-industrial transition and the spread of mass communications. Employing the postindustrial schema devised by Daniel Bell, however, Maisel adds a third stage. The increase in both societal specialization and service-based activities in postindustrial societies, he argues, requires more specialized media to serve homogeneous groups of affluent consumers with the leisure time to pursue their specialized interests (Maisel, 1973, pp. 159-170; see also Innis, 1950, 1951; Bell, 1973).[11]

The model of media development proposed by Merrill and Lowenstein also has three steps. Termed the "Elite-Popular-Specialized Curve," it suggests that all media progress from an elite stage serving the interests of society's empowered opinion leaders, to a popular phase in which they appeal to the masses of a nation's population, to a final specialized stage. Aimed at precisely definable and fragmented segments of the total population, the authors note that "the third and final stage of the EPS curve [occurs] when four factors coalesce: higher education, affluence, leisure and population size" (Merrill & Lowenstein, 1979, pp. 29-35).

Van Zuilen's model proposes a "life cycle" for both types of media and individual titles. As James Playstead Wood, a magazine historian and senior executive of Curtis Publishing, once wrote, "If, like a person, a magazine is an individual entity, like a man or woman, it has its vigorous youth, its settled middle years, exhaustion, and old age" (Wood, 1971b, p. 279).[12] Van Zuilen defines five stages (developmental, growth, maturity, saturation, and decline and death) and charts the positions of a variety of media on a steeply rising and then gently declining curve. In 1977, for example, pay television, was in the development stage; cable television was in the growth phase; paperback books and specialized magazines were mature; newspapers, women's magazines, and movies were at the saturation stage; black-and-white television was in decline; and traditional general interest, mass-audience magazines such as *Life* and *Look* were dead (Van Zuilen, 1977, pp. 275-286).

All these models are both descriptive and illustratively elegant. Like the silent workings of Aristotle's crystalline spheres, they suggest, if not a divine harmony, then a certain inevitability in the course of media growth and development. But models are, by definition, explanatory abstractions that extract patterns from greater forces and impose patterns on lesser details. Typically, their strength lies in their power to describe phenomena; their weakness, in their inability to identify causality. It can be argued that all these models share the weakness of failing to include: (a) larger sociocultural forces, including changing conceptions concerning the nature of personal identity and self-fulfillment; definitions of community and social roles; and the interrelated character of class, consumption, and leisure; and (b) the smaller operational considerations both within the industry and at individual enterprises; for example, the ability to define and appeal to specific audiences (readers) likely to be attractive to an identifiable group of prospective advertisers.

Interacting together, these two sets of factors may have been the critical determinants of the postwar success of the specialized magazine. And it is these factors—the pattern of larger forces driving social change, as well as the details of both changing industry norms and the specific magazine responses—that can help illuminate both America and its magazines since 1960.

## THE STRUCTURE

Because this study will attempt to portray the interaction between general social change and specific magazine-industry developments, its structure will approximate a pattern of alternation. In an effort to create a coherent fabric of argument, it will weave together three strands of inquiry: an examination of a number of larger historical forces, more detailed aspects of magazine history, and thematic considerations of social and cultural change. The outline for its seven chapters will conform to the following schema:

Chapter One, "Introduction," summarizes the study's thesis, as well as its interpretive premises and assumptions. Chapter Two, "Consensus Milieu, Consensus Magazines," describes the economic, social, and cultural transformation of America in the decade and a half following World War II and suggests how the character of the mass-circulation general magazines of the period reflected and reinforced the dominant values of the postwar period.

Chapter Three, "Changing Magazines in a Changing World," documents the historical demise of the mass-market publications and the rise of the special-interest magazines in the 1960s, and provides a history of early magazines devoted to specific leisure-activity interests. It discusses those somewhat anomalous general-interest titles that continued to prosper. It also outlines the internal economic elements (both in terms of advertising and circulation) that fostered the success of special-interest magazine publishing in the 1960s and summarizes the causes and effects of the changes in national marketing that occurred during this period.

Chapter Four, "The Other 1960s," addresses the external societal component of the equation. It both reviews the literature of relevant social theory and suggests that an important, largely unreported shift in values took place in the 1960s. Driven by affluence, rising education levels, and both an expansion and change in the meaning of leisure, many Americans sought to redefine themselves in terms of self, class, and community. One of the agents and by-products of that redefinition was the magazines they read.

Chapter Five, "The Knowledge Imperative," examines the media dimension of this value shift in some detail. It demonstrates, for example, how the special-interest magazines were able both to encourage and respond to the concerns of many readers related to individualism, social mobility and class status, generational issues, and loss of community. It also describes the founding of two special-interest magazines, *Boating* and *Car and Driver*, in the late 1950s and early 1960s, showing how their deliberate positioning to take advantage of the new realities of the time was essential to their success.

Chapter Six, "The Calculus of Success," examines the conceptual formulas concerning editorial tone, form, and content which many special-interest magazines used to appeal to their readers. It also discusses the magazine publishing industry's management norms and trade practices, with a particular emphasis on the relationships between the editorial, circulation, and advertising functions. Chapter Seven, "Conclusion," summarizes the key aspects of the study's evidence and arguments.

# 2

# CONSENSUS MILIEU, CONSENSUS MAGAZINES

AT FIRST THEY HAD ADVERTISED PARK FOREST AS HOUSING.
NOW THEY BEGAN ADVERTISING HAPPINESS.
  —WILLIAM H. WHYTE (1956, P. 258)

## POSTWAR PROSPERITY AND SOCIAL CHANGE

In the postwar years, America's magazine industry, led by the premier mass-market flagships, *Life*, *Look*, and the *Saturday Evening Post*, reflected the growing material assurance and satisfied consensus born of the triumph of World War II. From the very close of the conflict, most of the nation seemed imbued with all the relief, joy, and promise suggested by one of *Life*'s memorable V-J Day photographs.[1] In that anonymous sailor's celebratory Times Square embrace of the white-stockinged nurse, one can perhaps see not only the exhilaration of a war well won, but also the confidence of a people eager to grasp the promise of prosperity. "We had as a nation emerged from a great war, itself following upon a long and protracted Depression," wrote the psychologist Joseph Adelson. "We thought, all of us, men and women alike, to replenish ourselves in goods and spirit" (Adelson, 1972, p. 94).[2]

A robust industrial infrastructure and financial assets of unrivaled strength and size certainly made such replenishment possible after World War II. The result was a social transformation unmatched since the Industrial Revolution. As in that earlier reshaping of society, the engine of change was economic growth.[3] In the 15 years following the war, America's gross national product increased by 250%; consumption of personal services, 300%; and new construction, 900%. By 1960 per capita income was more than one third higher than even the boom year of 1945.[4]

Fueled by this extraordinary economic expansion, much of American society was transformed, and in the process the fabric of social reality itself was rewoven. In the tangible terms of the era, it is likely that most Americans believed that changes for the better had occurred. For many, virtually every aspect of material aspiration and social prospect was improved. Driven by the newly created wealth, marked societal change occurred in a number of interrelated dimensions. Matters of class and consumption, education, residence, and recreation were all affected. Each, in ways both direct and indirect, would be reflected in the character of the American magazine.[5]

Postwar prosperity almost doubled the proportional size of the middle class. In the last boom year before the Great Depression, 31% of the American people had achieved a middle-class standard of living (defined as a $3,000 to $10,000 income in 1955 dollars). By the mid-1950s, the percentage neared 60. Between 1947 and 1957 alone, the number of workers in the emerging managerial/professional/technical class rose 61%. Moreover, with the hardships of the Depression and the war behind them, Americans embraced an expanded ethos of consumption. Never before had so many been willing—and able—to consume so much. Encouraged by large, appealing advertisements in the glossy mass-market magazines, the fever of consumption was not only a consequence, but also an essential ingredient of prosperity. The initial postwar demand of cars, appliances, and new furniture soon expanded during the 1950s into mass consumption of lesser goods and services, including recreational products and leisure-related services.[6]

Economists of the period offered varying interpretations of the phenomenon. Walt Rostow of MIT, for example, announced with approval that the United States had entered the "high mass consumption" stage of economic development. Yale's James Tobin, however, when asked in 1958 the purpose of the extensive postwar investments in domestic production, replied: "For new consumer luxuries . . . all to be marketed by the most advanced techniques of mass persuasion to a people who already enjoy the highest and most frivolous standard of living in history" (cited in Matusow, 1984, p. 10). By the end of the decade, a respected economic historian could write: "The remarkable capacity of the U.S. economy in 1960 represents the crossing of a great divide in the history of humanity" (Vatter, 1963, p. 11).[7]

## LEARNING, LIVING, AND LEISURE

Spurred by the G.I. Bill, college enrollments soared. In 1946, 2 million students attended institutions of higher learning. By 1960, when the sociologist Daniel Bell wrote of the "knowledge revolution," enrollments approached 3.5 million, and by the end of that decade over 7 million students were in college. The new appetite for knowledge had many effects. For every professor who left a faculty, five replacements had to be hired. The number of new books published each year increased 65% between 1950 and 1960, and then doubled again in the 1960s. The rise in education also caused quantitative changes in the nation's occupational structure. Compared to the prewar totals, for example, by the mid-1960s the population of engineers had almost quadrupled, and the number of scientists had increased nearly 10 times. But there was a subtle qualitative evolution as well. "Knowledge, it was assumed, was not only power," the historian Godfrey Hodgson suggested, "but happiness as well" (Hodgson, 1976, p. 6).[8]

At the same time, where and how most Americans lived began to change. By the mid-1950s, 4,000 families a day were moving to the suburbs, and the national mobility rate increased by 50%. Within two decades the suburban population would double, and for the first time in the history of the world, a nation-state would contain more suburbanites than city dwellers or farmers. The only other comparable population shift in America's history was the influx of European immigration at the turn of the century. But as one study of the baby-boom generation noted, "More people moved to the suburbs every year than ever arrived on Ellis Island" (Jones, 1980, p. 43). Much of this national shift was due to the automobile. In the 30 years following 1950, while the U.S. population grew by 50%, the number of cars increased by 200%. The expanded automobility encouraged nonarterial settlement on the cities' outskirts, away from axes of public transportation. Moreover, the new land made possible lower housing densities and larger lot sizes. The result became the suburban standard, and whatever the cause of the nation's residential reorientation, Suburbia soon became synonymous with the American Dream.[9]

At least one additional aspect of social transformation, the changing role of leisure, characterized the postwar years. The advent of the eight-hour workday and five-day work week, as well as spreading affluence, made possible a marked increase in both leisure time and interest in recreation. It is possible that a new leisure ethic, strongly communal in nature, first emerged shortly after World War II. Martha Wolfenstein, a sociologist, observed that recreation began to replace work as early as 1950 as a means of expression and identity (Wolfenstein, 1958, pp. 86-97). Pierre Bourdieu, a French sociologist, would later note that it may also have been a manifestation of an ethos of, "as Parisians like to say, with a little shudder of audacity, *jouir*" (Bourdieu, 1984, p. 367).[10] During the 1950s, personal expenditures for recreation rose by 64%, from $11.1 billion to $18.3 billion, and economists calculated that, by the end of the decade, for every 1% increase in income, leisure consumption rose 1.3%.[11]

In the view of some, this burgeoning appetite for leisure may have been a mixed blessing. Intellectuals, in particular, found the trend disquieting. The Center for the Study of Leisure at the University of Chicago was established in the late 1950s to support scholarship giving voice to such concerns. "The most dangerous threat hanging over American society," warned the historian Arthur Schlesinger, Jr. in 1957, "is the threat of leisure . . . and those who have the least preparation for leisure will have the most of it" (cited in Swados, 1958, p. 359). The anthropologist Margaret Mead cautioned that leisure must serve the purposes of home and family life (Mead, 1958, pp. 10-15). "The primary problem for the future," wrote the sociologist David Riesman, "will be what to do with the surplus time and resources on our hands" (Riesman, 1964, p. 223).

Scholarly works with titles such as *Leisure in America: Blessing or Curse?* (Charlesworth, 1964) and *Work and Leisure: A Contemporary Social Problem* (Smigel, 1963) appeared. Many attempted to offer solutions to the questions posed by increased leisure; almost all regarded it as a problem. In *The Harried Leisure Class*, for example, Staffan Linder (1970), an economist, would later argue that affluence did not lead to a life of ease because of the press of time spent in leisure consumption itself. Similarly, cultural historians such as Warren Susman would write of the "pressure" of leisure time, noting that "homeowners in middle-class America . . . could not waste all this leisure. They had to use it up somehow" (Susman, 1989, p. 25).

Leisure, nonetheless, was a burden many American families were delighted to bear. With work assured, the economy expanded, producing new jobs and new wealth; play, particularly with family and friends, took on a new importance. Much of the new consumption focused on recreation, tripling the percentage of national income spent on leisure, from 4% before World War II to, by some estimates, 12% in the early 1960s. A combination of increased disposable income, a willingness to spend a substantial portion of it on recreation, significant improvements in leisure technology, and the success of mass-marketing techniques swelled the ranks of both traditional and, in the eyes of many at the time, somewhat novel pastimes.

As examples, the development and mass distribution of charcoal briquettes in the early 1950s were central to the widespread popularity of the backyard barbecue and the easy sociality it made possible. The sport of bowling benefited from shopping center locations, organized team play and tournaments, and the advent of automated pin-setting equipment; as a result, the number of bowling lanes in the nation more than doubled during the 1950s, and bowling enthusiasts rose from a prewar total of under 10 million to almost 30 million by 1960. During the 1950s, the demand for passports almost trebled (from 300,000 to 853,000) as more than 8 million Americans traveled abroad. And for those who stayed at home, a wealth of leisure pursuits—boating, skiing, photography, to name a few—began to compete for popular attention. A subtle attitudinal shift on the part of many Americans was also discernible: "We were moving into an era," one observer commented, "where there was an entitlement to leisure" (William Ziff, personal interviews, February 8, 1991; March 5, 1991; March 12, 1991).[12]

## THE AGE OF CONSENSUS

Viewed with neither a warm sense of nostalgia nor a cold shudder of distaste, it is clear that the 1950s were a time of unusual consensus and conformity. For many Americans, a Social Ethic had replaced the Protestant Ethic, and "belongingness" had become all important. Suburban families, especially younger ones, seemed animated by a need for community approval. "Friendliness" and "cooperation" were the watchwords, and most manifestations of personal eccentricity were discouraged.

The prevailing conformity may have had its price. As in the case of leisure, some observers thought it a dear one. Perhaps the most widely read contemporary critique was William H. Whyte's *The Organization Man*. Published in 1956, it was perhaps the most influential early statement of disillusionment by intellectuals with the suburban loss of individualism. David Riesman (1950, 1958) similarly wrote of "the suburban sadness" and "the lonely crowd." "The whole complex of suburban institutions represented a devastating blow to individuality, diversity and faith," wrote another commentator. "The 'social ethic' . . . simply represented an extension of the 'organization-man' style of cooperation. To get along, one had to go along. Individualism was forbidden" (Chafe, 1986, p. 121).

It would, however, be far from correct to suggest that the comfortable consensus of the 1950s did not have its defenders as well. In *Suburbia: Its People and Their Politics*, Robert C. Wood (1958) noted the existence of a new version of the Jeffersonian ideal. The critics who complained about conformity were described by Herbert Gans (1967) in *The Levittowners: Ways of Life and Politics in the New Suburban Community* as "largely upper middle class professionals, dedicated to cosmopolitan values and urban life and disdainful of the local and antiurban values of lower middle class and working class people" (p. 179). In *The Suburban Myth*, a survey of the literature on the subject, Scott Donaldson (1969) asserted that the 1950s suburban lifestyle had been "grossly and unfairly maligned" (p. vii). Later scholars such as Christopher Lasch (1977), noting the centrality of the family in the 1950s, argued for the usefulness of the social restraints of the period.

More recent scholarship also suggests that family life, both its internal dynamics and external concerns, may have been one of the crucial social determinants of the era. The success and stability of the traditional nuclear family so closely associated with the 1950s may, in retrospect, have been something of a historical anomaly. The high marriage and birthrates and stable divorce rates of the period were clearly a departure from the long-term demographic trends. "The patterns of family life characteristic of the fifties," Steven Mintz and Susan Kellogg (1988) observed in *Domestic Revolutions: A Social History of American Family Life,* "differed dramatically from any that has been observed earlier in our history or since" (p. 178). Andrew Cherlin (1981) noted that the Depression hardships and austerity of World War II could not fully explain the 1950s domesticity. "What was surprising was that years after this pentup demand for marriage and children should have been satisfied," he wrote in *Marriage, Divorce, Remarriage,* "the birth and marriage rates remained high" (pp. 34-35). Indeed, the annual birth rate continued to climb during most of the 1950s, peaking in 1957, more than a decade after World War II.

The resulting importance of the traditional family, as well as the roles it encompassed, was clearly defined. "The Victorian ideology of separate spheres was still partly intact; it was the husband's job to support the family, while the wife was the center of home life," wrote Francesca Cancian (1987, p. 37), a sociologist, in *Love in America: Gender and Self-Development.* Gender separation may, however, have been softened perhaps by the notion of family togetherness—of Mom, Dad, and the kids enjoying a backyard barbecue together. Despite the widespread readership of the Kinsey reports in the early 1950s, John D'Emilio and Estelle Freedman (1988) suggested in their definitive survey of American sexuality that conventional attitudes linking sex and morality dominated the decade.

Elaine Tyler May (1988) examined the connection between the ideology of the Cold War and conformist domesticity of the 1950s, arguing that they were two sides of the same coin: the need on the part of many Americans to feel both liberated from the past and secure about the future. The fundamental principle of the era, both politically and personally, she suggested in *Homeward Bound: American Families in the Cold War Era*, was containment, and in its domestic version, the primary "sphere of influence" was the home (p. 10). Similarly, other scholars noted that the underlying threat posed by atomic weapons themselves did much to define both the conformist tenor of postwar American culture and many people's need for familial security.[13]

Regardless of its underlying causes, it is clear that, for the rapidly expanding middle class, the consensual imperatives of the 1950s were indeed a central element of their Happy Days. "Whether you look at the writings of intellectuals or at the positions taken by practicing politicians or at the data of public opinion," wrote one historian, "it is impossible not to be struck by the degree to which the majority of Americans in those years accepted the same system of assumptions" (Hodgson, 1976, p. 67).[14]

## THE MASS MAGAZINES

It was those same assumptions that the major mass-circulation magazines of the era operated under—and underscored. The role of the magazine in this time of consensus was described, with approval, by James L.C. Ford (1969), a contemporary journalism scholar:

> The spacious lawn, shaded by flowering trees and cooled by the blue swimming pool, surrounds the split-level brick-and-white home. Turning smartly into the double garage is Dad, home from work and eager to get the barbeque going to begin the weekend relaxation. That's life for the affluent American family today, stimulated to a more luxurious, lively life by the home and family magazines. (p. 13)

Clearly, the major mass magazines of the period both reflected and promoted this satisfied, unruffled view of the world. *Life* Magazine, for example, devoted an entire issue in the late 1950s to "The Good Life," arguing in an editorial that by using their newfound affluence "to pursue true happiness, Americans can raise standards of excellence higher than anything in the world's past." The issue also carried a humorous piece on "the new leisure classes," which it labeled aristocrats, upper bourgeois, lower bourgeois, and peasants. Lest any readers, however, doubt the magazine's commitment to the egalitarian consensus of the age, an assurance was offered: "You should know it is not necessarily desirable to be an Aristocrat, or necessarily unpleasant to be a Peasant," the article's introduction read. "Your placement has little to do with any of the old standards of class distinctions—money, birth, breeding. What counts is simply how you spend your spare time." The same issue also included a selection of posed photographs of celebrities relaxing at their leisure: General Curtis LeMay fixing cars, Mrs. Mary Todd Rockefeller gardening, Alfred Knopf and Katherine Anne Porter in their kitchens, Edward Teller at the piano. The seven-page section had an obvious "just folks" theme, made all the more apparent by a notably contradictory element: August A. Busch Jr., the brewery heir, posing in front of the family mansion with a pet elephant.[15]

In the longer view, it can also be argued that centrality of the prevailing middle-class values to the mass magazines of the 1950s was clearly consistent with the historical origins of the modern magazine form. Prior to its emergence as a truly mass medium, most magazines served small, relatively elite, audiences. In the late nineteenth century, however, a number of societal factors—the success of the Industrial Revolution, the spread of public education and the subsequent rise in literacy, and the coalescence of a national consumer market—all contributed to the expansion of the American middle class, the essential mass audience for the new large-circulation magazines. Technological and commercial developments also played a major role. Economies of scale provided by new high-speed printing presses, improvements in photoengraving, distribution networks based on the newly completed national railroad system, and the advent of national advertising as a critical source of revenue all shaped the modern magazine form.[16]

Despite the early mass-market success of inexpensive "ten cent" magazines such as *Munsey's* (founded in 1889) and *McClure's* (1893), most magazine historians agree that the Curtis Publishing flagships of the early twentieth century, *Ladies Home Journal* edited by Edward Bok and George Horace Lorimer's *Saturday Evening Post*, served for the next 50 years as the dominant models of magazine development. Much of their success hinged on their capacity to underscore the mainstream values of their time. As a spokesman for the *Post* once observed, "It will, in time of turmoil and anxiety, be an expression of common sense. . . . If this sounds conventional or platitudinous, we would do well to remember . . . that truisms are true" (cited in Mooney, 1969, p. 73).[17]

In the view of some scholars of popular culture, the raison d'être of these early general-interest magazines was the promotion of a mass culture, and an essential element in that process was a conformist, consensus-building dynamic. "Success in the mass market," Stephen Holder (1972) wrote, "derives from providing a conforming rather than a transforming experience" (p. 88). By 1920, the *Post*, with 2,021,000 readers, and *Ladies Home Journal*, with 1,823,000, were the largest magazines in the United States. Buoyed by the increasing revenues derived from the mass advertising their huge circulations made possible, the magazines were in a position not only to mirror, but also in some measure to define contemporary cultural literacy for the newly created mass audience.[18]

The success of the mass-market schema, with the assumption and promulgation of shared values, was carried forward by a variety of publications during the first half of the 20th century. Notable examples included *Woman's Home Companion* and *Collier's*, which, like the Curtis titles above, had been originally established in the late 1800s. Others, such as *Reader's Digest, Time, Liberty, Life* and *Look*, were founded in the 1920s and 1930s.

In the decade and a half following World War II, the dominance of the general-interest, mass-market magazine seemed absolute, and both their advertising and editorial content reflected the consensual, communal spirit of the age. In *Magazines in the 20th Century*, Theodore Peterson (1956), a magazine historian, noted: "By playing on existing drives and attitudes in its attempts to sell goods and services, magazine advertising certainly reinforced many values of American society" (p. 389), which he characterized as material success, social conformity, and the need for social approval. Moreover, because the large mass-audience publications were predicated on a sense of national community, all had an editorial interest in perpetuating the status quo.

The entire contents of virtually all of the general-interest magazines of the period reflected this benign sense of contentment, this faith in the status quo. One particularly telling example, however, was an article that appeared in *Look* in early 1960. It included the results of a poll that suggested that most Americans "naturally expect to go on enjoying their peaceable, plentiful existence right through the Sixties and maybe forever" (Atwood, 1960, p. 11). As it turned out, for both America and its magazines, "forever" proved to be a surprisingly short span of time.

# 3

# CHANGING MAGAZINES IN A CHANGING WORLD

DEMOCRATIC NATIONS . . . WILL HABITUALLY PREFER THE USE-
FUL TO THE BEAUTIFUL.
—ALEXIS DE TOCQUEVILLE (1835/1956, P. 169)

## MAGAZINES IN THE 1960S

During the 1960s, the American consumer magazine industry completed a major transformation: a shift away from general-interest
mass-market publications toward more specialized magazines. Of
the nine prominent mass magazines listed at the conclusion of the previous chapter (*Collier's, Ladies Home Journal, Liberty, Life, Look, Reader's
Digest, Saturday Evening Post, Time,* and *Women's Home Companion*),
six had ceased publication by the early 1970s. Three principal causes led
to these failures: competition from television, mismanagement by publishing companies, and, as a less obvious but important undercurrent, an
inability on the part of some of the publications to respond to fundamental
sociocultural changes.

The late 1950s and early 1960s were a very difficult period for some publishing executives. "Many wondered if magazines were going to survive," recalled Robert Farley, executive vice president of Magazine Publishers of America (MPA), an industry trade group (personal interview, December 3, 1991).[1] Most of the general magazines had circulation and advertising strategies based on competition with television. But because television could create an audience at no cost, many magazines soon found their profit margins threatened. Many observers in the late 1950s suspected that television was going to be, in the words of Michael Hadley, former president of Times Mirror Magazines, "the bigger and tougher kid on the block" (personal interview, December 23, 1991). By the 1960s, the perception of broadcasting's comparative superiority in swaying mass audiences was certainly apparent, at least on the part of those with a pivotal influence on corporate advertising decisions. It was clear that television had become a glamorous medium. "The advertising agencies fell in love with it at the expense of magazines," said Archa Knowlton, director of media planning from 1958 to 1978 for General Foods, a major consumer advertiser. "It all sounds somewhat irrational, but every night advertising people went home, watched TV, and loved it. Few went home and read *Ladies Home Journal*" (personal interview, December 18, 1991; see also Jacoby & Hoyer, 1987).

It was widely believed that advertising on television worked differently from print ads. For mass marketers, television held out a promise even the largest magazine could not match: the power to create a nation of buyers. Everyone, it seemed, was watching the same thing. There was, moreover, a certain immediacy to its effect. "Run a commercial on Sunday night," said Gilbert Maurer, executive vice president of the Hearst Corporation, "and on Monday you would be inundated with customers" (personal interview, December 23, 1991). In addition, another reason for television's appeal as a national advertising medium was an early trade practice that remained in effect until the late 1960s. By agreement with the networks, major consumer-goods advertisers such as General Electric, Procter & Gamble, Westinghouse, and Kraft Foods were allowed to produce their own television shows, thus insuring their complete control over program content. "With shows like Danny Thomas, Andy Griffith, and Lucille Ball," recalled General Foods' Archa Knowlton with a degree of remembered pride, "we virtually *owned* Monday nights from 8:30 to 10:00 during 1960s" (personal interview, December 18, 1991).

Rapid improvements in broadcasting technology and reception quality added to the magazines' troubles. Of particular import was the advent of color television in the early 1960s, for the new technology meant that television could present vivid and attractive images which previously could only be displayed in magazines. The publishers' advertising representatives could no longer point out the shadowy limitations of their prospective clients' ads on black-and-white television. Once color commercials became possible, magazines as an advertising medium lost their last advantage.

It can be argued that, for many people in magazine publishing, television's sudden rise to prominence may have had psychological as well as economic effects. Magazines had been the primary national advertising medium since the late 19th century. Moreover, a select, highly visible group of mass magazines accounted for the vast majority of total circulation, with, by one estimate, 20 titles enjoying 80% of the circulation in the country. "After seventy-five years of dominance, we were suddenly being consigned to a lesser position by TV," said Donald Kummerfeld, president of the Magazine Publishers of America and former president of Murdoch Magazines. "There was shock and panic as magazines' share of market declined. We didn't know where the bottom was" (personal interview, December 23, 1991; see also Bogart, 1956, pp. 153-166).

In retrospect, the principal miscalculation in the management strategy of many mass magazines in the 1950s and 1960s seems to have centered on an unrestrained belief in the wisdom of ever-increasing circulation. It is perhaps worth noting that, for many of the most prominent publications, this strategy was a widely held article of faith well before the rise of television. "In the years following World War II," said Hearst's Gilbert Maurer, "there was a tacit agreement between the large advertising agencies such as Batten, Barton, Durstine, and Osborn and Young & Rubicam and publishers like Cowles and Curtis that, in placing its national advertising, American industry would buy all the 'reach' available" (personal interview, December 23, 1991). It was this unspoken business understanding, rather than any actual demand from the public, that may have driven much of the postwar circulation growth of magazines such as *Life, Look,* and the *Saturday Evening Post.*

Initially, the sale of the advertising space to national manufacturers to promote the postwar expansion of the consumer economy proved enormously profitable to the publishers. With a surfeit of advertising pages, it was possible for the magazines to "buy" circulation. The ethos of the 1950s was that a good circulator can sell anything at the right price. "Editors had little responsibility for their magazines' circulations," Maurer explained, "and in a palmy advertising climate, it is always easy to look good." The large advertising volumes allowed the mass magazines to make a profit from every additional unit of circulation, no matter what the additional readers cost them to acquire and renew (see Krishnan & Soley, 1987, pp. 17-23).

Few observers at the time, however, appreciated the degree to which many general-interest magazine publishers had leveraged themselves to obtain these large circulations. Like the junk-bond crisis of the late 1980s, maintaining the large circulations proved to be a huge obligation, one that would prove exceedingly difficult to meet—and still earn a profit—once television had arrived. "The wonderful money machine turned, in just a few years, into a loss-making machine. It became a tiger by the tail," a publishing official later noted (Maurer, personal interview, December 23, 1991). The reason for this was that the fundamental economics of publishing rewarded the raising of a magazine's circulation and severely penalized its lowering. In the calculus of matching circulation guarantees to advertising rates, a decrease in circulation not only meant lost circulation revenue; publishers were also required to pay back a portion of the advertising income to compensate the advertisers for the smaller audience for their ads. It is likely, in the management mindset of the time, that reducing circulation was never considered anything other than the option of the very last resort.

Indeed, with the emergence of television, the mass magazines, enamored of their large circulations, elected to try to fight it on the new medium's own ground. It was a clear case of mismanagement. "To increase their circulation, they gave away their magazines at a loss," said James Manousos, editor-in-chief of *Publishing Trends and Trendsetters*, an industry newsletter. "Circulation salesmen would get a bonus of fifty cents for every new subscription, so many would just sit down with a phone book and send in the names. *Look*, for example, had a lot of that circulation at the end" (personal interview, December 30, 1991).

Virtually giving their magazines away to maintain their circulations was not the only ploy the mass magazines used to compete with the ever-increasing audience offered to advertisers by television. Asserting that every copy of their publications was seen by an average of three or four readers, many also began to sell "total readership" rather than paid circulation. The basis of the claim was something called "syndicated research." Conducted by third-party firms hired by the magazine companies, these commercial surveys had as an unspoken but obvious objective the inflation of magazine readership numbers by including calculations for "pass-along" circulation. Also called "total-audience research," these syndicated studies actually originated in the early 1950s; one of the first survey firms involved was the A.C. Nielsen Company, which would later concentrate on serving the research needs of the television industry. By the 1960s, however, the studies that the large publishers needed to support claims of pass-along readership were being supplied by more sympathetic research firms such as W.R. Simmons Company and MRI, Inc. The magazines were not disappointed with the results provided. Though the *Saturday Evening Post's* paid circulation in the mid-1960s was approximately 6 million, it could claim a total audience, based on the pass-along surveys, of some 14 million readers. *Look's* 8 million circulation reportedly reached 18 million readers, and *Life*'s 7 million copies were, the studies asserted, read by 21 million people. Despite these inflated claims, the mass-circulation magazines clearly failed to meet the challenge of television's growing dominance as the mass advertising medium of choice. During the 1960s, television's share of the national advertising expenditures more than doubled, from $1.5 billion to over $3.5 billion. In contrast, magazine advertising revenues were relatively flat during the same period, rising from under $1 billion to $1.2 billion (Kinnear, Horne, & Zingery, 1986, pp. 261-270; Puliyel, 1986, pp. 115-124).

As many of the mass magazine's financial troubles worsened during the 1960s, a measure of recklessness may have tainted their management decision making. There is little evidence to suggest, however, that the prevailing gospel of ever-increasing circulations was ever seriously questioned. In 1969, for example, *Look*'s circulation briefly overtook that of *Life*. To celebrate its accomplishment, *Look* placed a full-page advertisement in the *New York Times*; the headline read: "*Look* is bigger than *Life*." Stung by the taunt and eager to regain its former status, *Life* quickly bought the subscriber list of the *Saturday Evening Post* when it folded later that year (Holder, 1972, pp. 78-89; Mooney, 1969, pp. 73-75). "This may have been the biggest mistake in the latter part of *Life*'s existence," a publishing executive remarked later. "No one should have touched that subscriber list" (Maurer, personal interview, December 23, 1991). Within a year, it was clear that the former *Post* readers were not renewing their subscriptions to *Life*, so the magazine had to spend *more* money to find *new* readers to maintain its enlarged rate base.

As the mass magazines continued to increase their circulations by any means possible in an attempt to compete with television, they also raised the prices they charged their advertisers. "After a while, the advertisers began to look more closely at what was going on," recalled one industry observer, "and they were not pleased" (Manousos, personal interview, December 30, 1991). Before long, the most serious of consequences became apparent: The number of advertising pages in the mass magazines suffered a marked decline. The annual total of advertising pages carried in *Life* Magazine, for example, decreased by almost 50% during the 1960s. Some national advertisers, however, tried to be sympathetic to the magazines' plight. Concerned about the geometric increases in broadcast advertising at the expense of print in the late 1960s, General Foods conducted an extensive marketing study to compare the relative merits of magazines and television as advertising vehicles; the test showed that the two media were equally effective in selling products. As a result, General Foods, as well as Procter & Gamble and a number of other large consumer advertisers, began to require that their agencies include magazines in all proposed advertising schedules. "We wanted," said General Foods' Archa Knowlton, "to allow magazines to compete with this monster that was devouring them."

The fundamental problem, however, of artificially inflated circulations remained. "We were concerned about the large magazines, particularly how they were maintaining their circulations," remembers Knowlton. "We'd look at the audited circulation reports and see newsstand sales falling, increases in discounted subscriptions, and a lot of arrears. We could see what they were doing to themselves." Perhaps by that time it was far too late for most mass magazine executives to change course. "When we'd bring up our concerns with them, they'd say, 'You stick to your business and we'll stick to ours'" (personal interview, December 18, 1991).

Beyond the evident economic and management considerations, it can also be argued that much of the trouble experienced by many mass-market magazines in the 1960s may have been due, in the words of the MPA's Robert Farley, to "their editorial failure to keep up with the changes in American society in the 1960s" (personal interview, December 3, 1991). According to social researchers, it was a decade of "new rules," and the social and cultural values inherent in, for example, a Norman Rockwell *Post* cover, *Liberty*'s "reading times," or another starlet pictorial in *Life* seemed clearly out of step with the times (Yankelovich, 1981).[2]

As reflectors and shapers of the widespread social consensus that defined postwar America until 1960, the mass-market magazines had great success with editorial personas that underscored the conformity of the age. They could indeed serve as "the best periodical measures of the concerns, the tastes, and the standards of an era," wrote the historian Theodore Greene (1970, p. 61). "In the 1950s, everyone wanted to wear the same clothes, drive the same car, live in the same house. Uniformity was not a bad thing," said one industry observer. "In fact, limited choice was seen as the key to American efficiency, and mass marketing, not the consumer, was king back then" (Kummerfeld, interview, 1991). In the view of some publishing executives, the editorial weaknesses of the mass magazines may have been suggested by a particular item in their circulation reports. (See Appendix, Table 1.) "As a magazine publisher, one way to gauge how well you are serving your readers' interests is single-copy sales on newsstands," said Gilbert Maurer of Hearst. "I think it is revealing that the paid circulations of *Life*, *Look*, and the *Saturday Evening Post*, for example, all had less than five percent newsstand sales. During their circulation run-ups in the 1960s, they clearly lost sight of what the American public wanted to read" (personal interview, December 23, 1991).

## THE RISE OF THE SPECIALIZED MAGAZINE

As many of the mass-circulation publications suffered, magazines addressing the specific interests of specific readers prospered. Between 1955 and 1965, the circulations of a wide variety of more targeted publications enjoyed significant growth. For instance, the readership of *Boy's Life* and *Sports Illustrated* doubled during this period, *Mechanix Illustrated* and *Scientific American* almost tripled in size, and the circulation of *Playboy*, certainly a special case, increased tenfold.[3]

A number of factors may have contributed to the process of specialization in U.S. magazines during the 1960s. In economic terms, major advances in printing technology that not only lowered costs but changed the economies of scale were critically important. The computerization of both typesetting and color-separation processes, as well as the advent of compact, high-quality offset presses, resulted in reduced per-copy manufacturing costs. Large print runs were no longer necessary, and small circulation magazines suddenly became more profitable. (See Appendix, Table 2.) With production costs falling, it became possible to produce smaller magazines for specialized audiences. "This was," said James Manousos of *Publishing Trends*, "a more 'natural' way to distribute information. It was also a change in the economics that has been a normal development in every communications medium" (personal interview, December 30, 1991; see also Schmidt, 1980, pp. 3-16).

In his thoughtful book, *The Power to Inform*, the media critic Jean-Louis Servan-Schreiber suggested a variety of social changes that influenced the trend toward specialized diversity in magazines. A general increase in social tolerance may have allowed the greater assertion of new freedoms and tastes. This, along with the postwar rise in levels of education which helped to create a multiplicity of personal interests, produced new, smaller social groupings which smaller, more specialized magazines could effectively address. Increased affluence, moreover, made even smaller potential magazine markets financially feasible as business propositions, particularly those related to the rising interest in leisure activities (Servan-Schreiber, 1978, pp. 36-38).[4]

Despite the troubles of many large-circulation magazines, the total number of periodicals rose in the 1960s from 8,422 to 9,573 titles, and personal expenditures on periodicals increased from $2.1 billion to $3.4 billion. (See Appendix, Tables 3-5.) As a result, a wide assortment of magazines targeted at specific subjects flourished. In some cases, established magazine genres particularly benefited; both religious periodicals of all denominations and "handyman" magazines for the do-it-yourselfer proliferated. In others, whole new categories of special-interest magazines emerged. These included a new breed of city/regional magazine, largely modeled on Clay Felker's *New York* (founded in 1967 as an insert in the *World Journal Tribune*, a newspaper) which was both journalistically aspiring and service-oriented, and a wide variety of psychological awareness and self-improvement magazines such as *Psychology Today* (1966) (U.S. Department of Commerce, 1975, p. 810; U.S. Department of Commerce, 1980, p. 204; see also Board, 1990, pp. 119-142; Fletcher, 1977, pp. 740-743; Menon, Bush, & Smart, 1987, pp. 14-20). Particularly notable was the success enjoyed by magazines focused on active leisure pursuits. Described by one contemporary observer as a "revolutionary boom," participatory sports burgeoned during the 1960s. Personal expenditures on recreation more than doubled during the decade, increasing from $18.3 billion to $40.7 billion. Similarly, the number of books published about sports and recreation also doubled from 233 titles in 1960 to 583 in 1970 (U.S. Department of Commerce, 1975, pp. 316-318, 808).

At least two other factors favored the special-interest magazine publishers of the 1960s. First, a study examining the period from 1946 to 1977 suggested that, although the loyalty of readers to newspapers had been declining since the 1950s, magazine readership, especially among the young, continued to climb steadily during the period, despite the popularity of television. (See Appendix, Table 6.) Second, rather than competing with the time individuals spent reading, it appeared that leisure activities merely whetted the appetite of many for more printed information about their avocational pursuits. (See Appendix, Table 7.) The more compelling their interest, the more likely they were to want to read more about it (McEvoy & Vincent, 1980, pp. 134-140; Robinson, 1980, pp. 141-152).

As a result, by the early 1960s, a number of newspaper and broadcasting companies saw the potential in special-interest magazine publishing. The Hearst Corporation set the precedent, and was soon followed by Times Mirror, CBS, the *New York Times*, and ABC. Some started new magazines; others bought existing titles. This "multimedia-ization" dramatically changed special-interest publishing, transforming what had been a number of small separate cottage industries into big, quite competitive businesses. "We were up against companies such as Ziff-Davis and Petersen, which were dedicated solely to special-interest magazine publishing," said Michael Hadley, former president of Times Mirror Magazines, "and the competition was intense" (personal interview, December 23, 1991).

The rewards for success in the competition were considerable. The Ziff-Davis Publishing Company, for example, concentrated its efforts on consumer magazines aimed at aviation, automotive, boating, photography, and skiing enthusiasts. Its titles, each the dominant entry in its category, included *Flying, Car and Driver, Boating, Popular Photography*, and *Skiing*, as well as *Cycle, Popular Electronics*, and *Stereo Review*. During the decade of the 1960s, the circulation of its magazines grew by an annual average of almost 10%, its gross revenues more than doubled, and its profits increased more than 15 times.[5] (See Appendix, Tables 8-11.)

Similar gains were realized by other publishers who chose to apply themselves to the leisure-oriented special-interest magazine genre: Hearst, Times Mirror, Petersen, the New York Times Company, and both ABC's and CBS's magazine subsidiaries. In contrast, the companies that published three of the four most celebrated postwar general-interest publications, *Look*, the *Saturday Evening Post* and *Collier's*, were soon out of the consumer magazine business altogether.

In an industry as diverse and decentralized as magazine publishing, however, it would not be accurate to suggest that these two trends of the 1960s, the precipitous decline of the large general-interest publication and the sudden rise of the leisure-active specialized magazine, were historical absolutes. Though often considered in a class by itself, *Reader's Digest* was certainly a mass-audience publication, and during the 1960s its U.S. circulation grew from 13 million to almost 18 million.[6] Similarly, during this period a number of other specialized magazine genres unrelated to recreational pursuits also thrived. Despite competition for advertising from television in some cases, the newsweeklies, the city/regional magazines, business and financial publications, television programming guides, and women's "service" magazines covering home and fashion all prospered. Publications aimed specifically at women, for example, flourished during the 1960s, and during the decade 5 of the 10 largest magazines in America (*Ladies Home Journal*, *McCall's*, *Family Circle*, *Better Homes & Gardens*, and *Good Housekeeping*) were women's magazines. Nevertheless, the proliferation and success of what had previously been called, somewhat derisively, the "hobby books" were significant markers of the era.

It is also worth noting that leisure-active publications as a genre had existed long before the 1960s. One of the magazine categories with the longest history, outdoor or "sporting" journals, had blossomed shortly after the Civil War. By the turn of the century there were more than 50 such magazines, most of which were gentlemen's journals celebrating "the sporting life" and devoted to hunting, fishing, horse racing, and other outdoor activities. Some wielded significant social and political influence in their day. *Forest and Stream*, for example, established in 1873, was the force behind the founding of the Audubon Society, whereas *Appalachia*, established three years later, was instrumental in the passage of the Congressional act that created the national forests. During the 1930s, however, many of these journals declined, the result of the Great Depression's hardships and changing social tastes, and only three major titles, *Field & Stream*, *Outdoor Life*, and *Sports Afield*, were in a position to benefit in the larger postwar boom in recreation-centered special-interest magazines (Mott, 1938, Vol. 3, pp. 210-211).[7]

## A MARKETING REVOLUTION

Two requirements were—and to this day continue to be—essential for long-term success in magazine publishing: (a) specific information in a specific form that can be expected to appeal to a definable segment of readers; (b) a group of manufacturers or distributors with the means and willingness to advertise their products and services to those readers. One of the most important aspects is the perceived level of reader commitment to a magazine's subject. "The key is that the special-interest publications demand high reader involvement—subscribers are participants in the subject being written about," wrote the media scholar Benjamin Compaine. "Thus the special-interest magazine is selling a readership of unquestionable homogeneity . . . while providing a waiting audience with sought-after information that often results in intense cover-to-cover reading of editorial and advertising content alike" (1980, p. 103).

"Some companies like Ziff-Davis were very successful in developing specialized magazines targeted at recreational activities," said James Manousos. "It was good business because, with 'generic' advertisers so well defined, one could get in for less. And with so little 'wasted' circ, you could charge your advertisers more" (personal interview, December 30, 1991). Because they dealt with a single product or activity that was fundamental not only to the editorial material but also to the bulk of advertising, specialized magazines could deliver a specific, highly defined audience to their advertisers.

Most successful special-interest magazines relied on a fairly simple editorial formula that supported both these requirements. The basic tenets concerning editorial content included: an unremitting focus on non-fiction rather than fiction; product rather than "people" articles; a participatory, hands-on tutorial rather than vicarious approach to all subjects; and a high degree of technical complexity. More important perhaps than simply serving the informational needs of some readers, all of this was designed to attract the specific kinds of deeply committed readers, "heavy users" in the parlance of publishing, whom potential advertisers would find attractive. "People had long read what were once called 'fan' publications, but in the 1960s it became clear that people who read our special-interest magazines wanted to buy things," recalled one magazine executive. "We were always amazed by our purchasing studies. Our readers accounted for seventy percent of all high-quality, high-priced products sold, roughly $1000 a year. So for advertisers, the people they wanted to reach with their ads selected themselves by reading our magazines" (Furman Hebb, former executive vice-president, Ziff-Davis Publishing, personal interview, February 1, 1991).

An interesting aspect of this equation was the practice of subtly discouraging less-committed readers unattractive to advertisers. "We scared away the readers we didn't want by intimidating them," said William Ziff, chairman of Ziff-Davis Publishing. "They either weren't competent to read it technically, or they weren't competent to read it in terms of ideational or vocabulary complexity." As an added benefit, this exclusionary approach lowered the companies' circulation promotion costs. "Our attitude was that we didn't want everyone to subscribe. So we saved our money, and instead simply said: 'Here it is. If you don't already know about it, you're not going to subscribe anyway'" (Ziff interview, February 8, March 5, and March 12, 1991).[8]

Fortuitously, the ability of special-interest magazines to deliver finely targeted, high-consuming audiences to advertisers coincided with two major transformations in consumer marketing. First, many postwar brands of consumer goods had become well established by 1960. As a result, the goal of much national advertising began to shift from image creation and brand recognition to more closely fought contests of market share. One implication of this was that advertising had to appeal to more knowledgeable customers than in the immediate postwar years. To accomplish this, many ads began to provide more information, rather than simply selling "image."

At the same time, advances in computer technology, as well as reductions in its price, led to a second trend: the evolution of proprietary research in market segmentation by lifestyle, attitudes, and behavior. "It is important to remember that media planning before about 1960 was an emotional thing," recalled one media planner. "Ads in *Life* were bought and sold over drinks at the Stork Club in those days. People at the advertising agencies would decide what they wanted to do, and then simply build a rationale for it" (Archa Knowlton, personal interview, December 18, 1991). At first, the magazines themselves seemed to understand best targeted marketing; this was, after all, one of the few advantages they had over television. "The media were most influential in teaching advertisers how to do things differently," James Manousos recalled. "They taught the advertising world how to advertise." As a result of these efforts by the special-interest publishers, specificity of audiences came to be accepted by the ad agencies, and soon the driving force was the large national advertising agencies such as J. Walter Thompson, Young & Rubicam, and Ogilvy & Mather. "Few clients back then had their own research departments," one analyst remembered, "so the agencies competed with each other on the basis of the uniqueness of the research they could offer" (Paul Chook, vice-president, marketing, Ziff Communications, personal interview, December 21, 1990).

The result was a marketing revolution: from inventing a product and then finding customers for it to first studying one's customers and then making what they wanted. Early attempts at targeted marketing were crude. Gender was the first differentiation, because certain advertisers decided they primarily wanted to reach women. Soon new research techniques were developed to study not just the demographics of audiences, but their psychographics as well. Employing only the gross demographic categories might, for overstated example, lead one to presume that Phyllis Schlafly and Gloria Steinem were similar customers, or that Grace Slick of Jefferson Airplane and Tricia Nixon Cox, or perhaps Anita Bryant and Renee Richards, could be reached with the same advertisement. However, by using more revealing variables such as educational level, residential zip code, and occupational status, customer characteristics could be far more sharply defined.

Some of the large consumer-goods companies embraced targeted marketing with a passion. "We developed our own computerized media planning system in 1961, one of the first in the industry," recalled Archa Knowlton. It allowed General Foods to match the demographics of magazines and television shows by age, income, marital status, and geography with the target audience for specific products. The proprietary software also assigned a 'persuasion value' to each specific medium for each product; for example, a Jello ad would be more effective in a culinary magazine than in a men's magazine. "Remember, this was the early 1960s. It took our computer fifty hours of processing to produce the printout. It was the damndest thing you ever saw" (Knowlton interview, December 18, 1991).

The rise of narrowly focused marketing clearly favored the position of special-interest magazines in the 1960s as advertising vehicles. Of particular importance was their appeal to upscale males, a market segment that national advertisers had traditionally found difficult to reach. As a result, the magazines were able to raise dramatically their advertising rates, in some cases more than tripling them during the course of the decade. (See Appendix, Tables 8-11.)

The price of advertising is usually expressed in terms of "cost per thousand" (cpm) readers or viewers. For magazines, the cost is that of a black-and-white advertisement, one full page in size; for television, a 30-second commercial. At the beginning of the 1960s, the cpm's of the special-interest magazines, though three times larger than network television's, were still below those of newsmagazines such as *Time* and *Newsweek*. By the end of the decade, their cpm advertising rates were twice those of the newsweeklies, and eight times the size of television's.[9] "If one understands the difference between incremental and average costs of production," one special-interest magazine official remarked with remembered satisfaction, "one can perhaps appreciate what that did for our profitability" (Hebb interview, February 1, 1991).

By the end of the 1960s, the transformation of the consumer magazine industry was virtually complete. Victims of television's ascendancy and their own mismanagement, many mass-audience magazines had failed. In their place, a wide variety of specialized magazines were flourishing. The evolution of both targeted marketing techniques by major advertisers and of publishing technology contributed to their development, and many magazine publishers eagerly established new and expanded existing special-interest titles, particularly those concerned with active leisure activities.

In a broader sense, however, the success of the special-interest magazines in the 1960s was also due to a number of concurrent sociocultural changes. Many Americans, it seemed, wanted to pursue new means of self-expression, to devote themselves to new, more individualistic interests, perhaps to reinvent themselves. This was the need that many of the specialized magazines served, and it was this yearning that largely defined what might be called "The Other 1960s."

# 4

# "THE OTHER 1960s"

THE REAL CYCLE YOU'RE WORKING ON IS THE CYCLE CALLED "YOURSELF."
—ROBERT PIRSIG (1974, P. 99)

## THE AMORAL MAJORITY?

As the total personal income of Americans rose 70% during the 1960s, there was ample evidence of a soaring individualistic interest in leisure pursuits, not least of which was the flowering of specialized magazines designed to serve and further develop those very interests. Less apparent, however, were the underlying sociocultural influences that may have shaped the trend.

Individualism in various forms had long been a central aspect of American society. Early observers such as Hector Crèvecoeur in *Letters from an American Farmer* (1780) and Alexis de Tocqueville in *Democracy in America* (1835) regarded it as one of the distinguishing features of the American character. It can be argued that the somewhat self-indulgent individualism that emerged in 1960s had, at least in part, its origins in the social conformity of the 1950s. Perhaps the pious repetitions of consensus, community, and social discipline did not square with an economic system based on frivolous consumption and material gratification. Indeed, within a few years, mainstream middle-class values would be disapprovingly characterized by some scholars and social critics as "a culture of narcissism" (Crèvecoeur, 1904; Lasch, 1977; Matusow, 1984, p. 306; Tocqueville, 1956).

It is also possible that the widely reported harmony and somnolent uniformity of the 1950s were, at least in part, deceptive. Many intellectuals, writers, and artists, as well as others, found the conformity of the era painfully repressive. Before the decade was half over, a young Norman Mailer, just assuming his role as one of the more quotable spokesmen for the world of literature, was moved to call it "the worst decade in the history of man" (1954, pp. 358-359).[1] Evidence of some of the cultural contradictions of the 1950s can also be found in the performing arts. Although Hollywood offered Doris Day and Rock Hudson as paragons of docile domesticity and conventional cuteness, James Dean and Marlon Brando may have been the more significant stars of the decade. The celebrity of these unconventional and rebellious figures certainly had a notable intensity, and it is probable that their public appeal was due, to large extent, to an underlying resonance with the unrevealed passions of the time. "It is intriguing to ponder," wrote the social historian Jackson Lears, "the complexity of the personal conflicts that must have existed inside all those allegedly identical houses in the suburbs" (1989, p. 52).[2] More recently, Robert Schickel, the cultural critic, could write:

> In truth, there was something abnormal about 1950s normalcy. What was clear to a few social commentators—and is evident to anyone looking back on that decade now—was that the great '50s consensus was, in the largest sense, a fraud. On most important matters—relationships between the races, sexes, classes and generations, for example—it grotesquely misrepresented reality. (1990, pp. 18-19)

Whatever the exact nature of the 1950s, the turmoil of 1960s ushered in marked social, political, and cultural change. Two aspects among the many can serve as thematic bookends for the decade, for their implications ranged from the subject of birth to a matter of death. On May 11, 1960, the first oral contraceptive was approved for sale by the U.S. Food and Drug Administration, and within five years it was estimated that perhaps a third of America's young women were on the Pill. The 1960s were also the decade of the Vietnam War. Of the 27 million young men of that generation, 40% were called to arms (of whom one quarter were draftees), and 57,000 perished by the war's end in the mid-1970s, but some 500,000 men chose criminal resistance or draft evasion to avoid involvement (Spencer, 1966, p. 22; see also Baritz, 1990).

But just as the consensus of the 1950s may have been less than complete, representing the 1960s as a time frothed with protest, sexual and political liberation, alternate lifestyles, and radical political reform may tell less than the whole story. Despite the tumult of the era, the demographer Daniel Yankelovich wrote that "the vast majority of Americans . . . [went] about their daily routines unruffled, their outlook on life hardly touched by these momentous happenings" (1981, p. xiii).

A number of commentators, particularly those on the Left, would later choose to characterize the 1960s as a time of moral generosity and political and communal action when concerted effort to correct civilization's ills and inequities seemed a real possibility.[3] There is, however, evidence to suggest that this interpretation, although attractive in its reformist sentimentality, may have failed to encompass some of the larger social realities of the era. National opinion polls during the Vietnam War, for example, clearly revealed that a majority of the population regarded the antiwar protesters with more distaste than the war itself. Similarly, more than two thirds of all Americans thought the city's security measures at the 1968 Democratic convention in Chicago were justified, and 57% believed that the police and National Guard had not used excessive force against the rioters. And despite widespread press coverage at the height of their popularity in the late 1960s, it is unlikely that back-to-the-land communes ever numbered more than 500; their estimated average membership was 20.[4]

It can be argued, nonetheless, that the 1960s did indeed represent a profound sociocultural value shift, away from socially defined and toward self-defined organizing principles. According to Daniel Yankelovich, a set of "new rules" had replaced the older verities largely based on one's fixed place in society. "For thirty years after the onset of the Depression, the need for economic security was paramount, and people didn't take anything for granted," said Donald Kummerfeld of the Magazine Publishers of America. "By 1960, however, the haunting ceased. We had both economic self-confidence and the realization that American values weren't homogeneous. Home, mother, God, and hard work were no longer the watch words" (Kummerfeld interview, December 23, 1991; see also Yankelovich, 1981).

In 1957, the U.S. Joint Commission on Mental Health asked the Survey Research Center at the University of Michigan to conduct a national study of Americans' sense of well-being and mental health. A follow-up survey, funded by the National Institute of Mental Health, was undertaken in 1976. The results of the two studies were compared by a team of psychologists led by Joseph Veroff. In *The Inner American: A Self-Portrait from 1957 to 1976*, they wrote: "There has been a shift from a socially integrated paradigm for structuring well-being, to a more personal and individuated paradigm" (Veroff, Douran, & Kulka, 1981, p. 529). It was apparent that sometime in the early 1960s, the communal values and social discipline had been superseded, and the new ethos was an expression of the demand by many for expanded personal freedom and self-fulfillment.[5]

The commercial implications of this change in values did not go unnoticed. "There was no doubt about it from an advertising perspective," recalled John O'Toole, president of the American Association of Advertising Agencies and former chairman of Foote, Cone & Belding, a prominent advertising agency. "The 1960s clearly were a time of both individualism and perhaps a distrust of largeness" (personal interview January 7, 1992). One result was a proliferation of discretionary activities and products, and with it, a new ethos: Maybe it wasn't wrong to indulge yourself. Maybe we had enough money to spend. Other observers in the media business noted the value shift. "By 1960, people had begun to 'arrive' and were looking for ways to spend their income. For those with the money and time to indulge themselves, it was the American dream," said Gilbert Maurer of Hearst. Indeed, it is possible that many Americans felt far less affinity for the political activism of the 1960s than was widely assumed at the time. "In some ways, that generation was as apolitical as any ever to come along," Maurer continued, "and perhaps part of the disaffection later in the decade arose simply from having the luxury of being able to look at our navels" (personal interview, December 23, 1991).

By the "Me Decade" of the 1970s, the ostentatious loss of self-denial represented cause for serious concern to some observers. "American capitalism has lost its traditional legitimacy, which was based on a moral system of reward rooted in the Protestant sanctification of work," wrote the sociologist Daniel Bell. "It has substituted a hedonism which promises material ease and luxury, yet shies away from all the historic implications of a 'voluptuary system,' with all its social permissiveness and libertinism" (1976, p. 84). At a minimum, the more individualistic, less consensual outlook represented a conflict of values. America was rediscovering itself, and one of its rediscoveries was that we were not a homogeneous nation. "The new values, which had been psychologically and sociologically suppressed, had an impact in the 1960s on both our attitudes and what we wanted to read," said Donald Kummerfeld. "And as society became more complex, it was clear that magazines would become more specialized" (personal interview, December 23, 1991; see also Hague, 1964; Hartshorne, 1968).

## THE TRIUMPH OF SELF

The shift during the 1960s to more individually defined values had a number of interesting societal implications. As large numbers of middle-class Americans attained the means and time to devote themselves to more private pursuits, many of the traditional notions of self, community, consumption, leisure, and class underwent significant change.

Any consideration of the social constructs underlying the rise of individualism in the 1960s—as well as its manifestation in the magazines of the period—must first address what some critics have seen as scholarly prejudice. "Confusion about the meaning of self-development partly explains the negative bias of academics. They link the search for self-fulfillment with extreme independence and self-indulgence," wrote Francesca Cancian (1987). "Lacking a clear social theory of the self, sociologically inclined scholars often dismiss the whole enterprise of self-development as another destructive, misleading product of capitalism" (p. 105).[6]

Karl Marx (1964, pp. 132-146), in fact, was one of the seminal thinkers on the subject of self-development. In his early writings, he acknowledged that all social laws are, by definition, repressive. In his view, it was essential that people be free to develop their individual potential, and he presented the somewhat idealistic argument that mankind would, if unoppressed by class, create a harmonious society through "natural love." Marx also thought it commendable—indeed, hoped—that greater political empowerment and a broader range of personal and economic choices would result in individual self-development. More recently, historians have suggested that the foundations of the modern sense of self arose from the travails of the late 19th century. Eli Zaretsky (1976, pp. 30, 69), in *Capitalism, the Family and Personal Life,* argued that it was in the 1880s that the first separation occurred between the outer world of alienated labor and the inner world of personal feeling. Aided by an increase in leisure time, this private sphere fostered need for self-gratification among common people, and the result was a democratization of the ethic of personal fulfillment that had previously been limited to elites. It is clear that, at least since the Industrial Revolution, there has been a marked, though uneven, expansion in both the possibility and reality of "personhood" for many Americans. "The multiple opportunities for self-definition and expression," wrote the social historian Peter Clecak (1983) in his wide-ranging study of the subject, *America's Quest for the Ideal Self: Dissent and Fulfillment in the 60s and 70s,* meant "a significant increase in available cultural space and a healthy thickening of individuality" (pp. 8, 25).

Other scholars have usefully noted both the role of work and gender in the emerging primacy of self. The influential social functionalist Talcott Parsons (1966) contrasted the emotionally expressive possibilities of personal life with the standards of rationality and performance which define most work. The psychologist Carol Gilligan (1982) underscored what she believed to be the gender aspects of self-development, focusing on men's apparent need to be instrumental and independent.

It can indeed be argued that there was a significant gender dimension to intensification of concern with self during the period. Certainly one of the most evident expressions—and one that was central to the rise of special-interest magazines—was male leisure interests. In the 1950s, wrote the social historian Peter Stearns (1990, pp. 165, 192, 197), men did raise "the leisure ante." They used their avocational interests not only to fill the expanding amount of leisure time available to them, but also as a major source of personal identity. Another gender factor, moreover, might also be considered: The rise of the suburbs, with their prevailing ethos of familial domesticity, as well as the postwar decline of traditional male clubs and bars, left many middle-class males without a source of gender solidarity. As a result, many sought a privatization of leisure through more individual recreational sports and hobbies.[7]

To some observers, this may have had an evolutionary basis. In *Men in Groups*, the anthropologist Lionel Tiger (1969) suggested that a "natural" male bonding developed as a result of the need for cooperative hunting in prehistoric times. Whatever its origins, the locker-room camaraderie so characteristic of other patterns of male association certainly must have been an important aspect of many men's leisure activities. Similarly, the literary scholar Leslie Fiedler (1966), in *Love and Death in the American Novel*, explored the possible cultural origins of men at play. In his analysis, the essential novelistic myth of American culture was the adventure of a young man who escapes from society to a womanless wilderness to enjoy violent exploits with a male companion. When one considers the appeal of the adventurous fellowship offered by recreations such as yachting or motor racing, Fiedler's cultural insights become highly suggestive.

The increasing importance of personal life was no doubt caused by a number of factors. Widespread affluence raised many Americans' living standards, extended educational opportunity, increased the time available for leisure activities, and facilitated occupational, geographical, and social mobility. There was, moreover, an important commercial element in the cultural equation. The thriving consumer culture and accompanying proliferation of media of the period certainly underscored the value of self-gratification as one of the central imperatives of a consumer society. In one interpretation, consumer advertising, with its persistent encouragement of individual consumption, may have reinforced the need for the individual to look out for himself. "Self-interest becomes the social norm, even duty," wrote the economist Fred Hirsh (1976) in *Social Limits to*

*Growth.* As many people began to place an increasing premium on their time, traditional forms of sociability and community were eroded and diminished. This erosion was deepened by the pervasive influence of consumer advertising and what Hirsch termed "the self-interest ethos of the market" (pp. 82, 84).

A more general sense of well-being may have also played a part. An increase in economic security often seemed to promote a heightened interest in new personal needs. As many Americans began to value individual self-development and independence rather than obedient conformity to well-defined social roles, many people felt confident enough to consider new directions and new sources of meaning in their personal lives. It is worth noting, moreover, that this impulse was not confined solely to middle-class Americans. In an interesting study of working-class values, the anthropologist George Spindler (1977, p. 34) also found clear evidence for an emphasis on independence, personal fulfillment, and personal competence.[8]

The emphasis on self-fulfillment was decidedly hastened by the fluid social circumstances of the late 1950s and early 1960s. Widespread economic security, a growing emphasis on youth and its challenges to traditional sexual mores, the move by many families from conventional urban neighborhoods to the more anonymous suburbs, increases in both educational opportunity and available leisure time, and, not least, a proliferation of both print and broadcast media, all contributed to the processes of social change. By the 1960s, it was clear to many observers that a major boundary of social organization may have been crossed. One way to define that boundary was the emerging primacy of the individual. "We had passed," wrote one sociologist, "from an era in which people's private lives were regulated by the obligations of family roles into a new era of the self" (Cancian, 1987, pp. 37-38).[9] A variety of national studies appeared to support the proposition. The psychologist Joseph Veroff and his colleagues (Veroff, Douran, & Koulka, 1981) noted that between the 1950s and the 1970s the importance of social standards and roles had diminished, whereas self-expressiveness and self-direction had increasingly become the focus of social life. In the early 1970s, the social researcher Daniel Yankelovich (1974) conducted a poll of college-age youth across the nation; it suggested that their primary goal was "finding just the right life style for expressing their psychological potential" (pp. 21-22).

In a sense, this new-found focus on self could have been viewed as an appropriate response to a widespread liberal scholarly distaste for the 1950s, an era, according to David Riesman (1950) when a nation of conformers had failed to heed its inner voice. The new, less conformist values, however, were not lacking in academic critics. One of the more widely noted was Christopher Lasch, who contended that the prevalent individualism was an unwelcome by-product of capitalism. In *The Culture of Narcissism* (1978), he claimed that individualism was also largely responsible for the loss of legitimate social authority and restraint, and a principal agent of victimization in capitalist society.[10] The sociologist Robert Bellah later headed a team of researchers which conducted extensive surveys of a variety of contemporary middle-class lifestyles. "Individualism may have grown cancerous," they wrote in *Habits of the Heart: Individualism and Commitment in American Life.* The essence of the problem was that "the meaning of one's life for most Americans is to become one's own person. Much of this process . . . is negative, [involving] breaking free from family, community, and inherited ideas" (Bellah, Madsen, Sullivan, Swidler, & Tipton, 1985, pp. vii, 82-83).[11] Unfortunately, their interpretation may have been based on a somewhat romanticized view of the past; as a result, they did not fully consider why, for many Americans, traditional notions of family, community, and inherited ideas were no longer appealing.

The threat of individualism to society's essential coherence had long been a concern of sociologists. Emile Durkheim (1951), one of the founders of modern sociology, argued that people must have strict social rules to limit their desires, restrain their emotions, and give their lives meaning. Similarly, the sociologist Ferdinand Tönnies (1940) wrote of the transition from warm, family-centered community relationships (Gemeinschaft) to a colder, more modern Gesellschaft in which each individual is isolated by himself (p. 38). To Tönnies and other loss-of-community theorists, modernization, urbanization, social mobility, and the decline of traditional beliefs were a clear sign of communal decay.[12] Perhaps the most expansive contemporary condemnation of individualism was offered by the social moralist Philip Rieff (1966). Disapproving of what he considered the substitution of individualism for faith in a collective morality, Rieff emphasized the importance of obedience to authority. Only through such a commitment, he wrote, could individuals achieve "those communal purposes in which alone the self can be realized and satisfied" (p. 4).[13]

These critics of individualism and the search for self-fulfillment, however, often seemed to consider only its troubling effects, while ignoring its variety, its vitality, and its effectiveness. Much of the criticism, moreover, reflected both a nostalgic, romanticized interpretation of the past and a somewhat authoritarian or "top-down" view of social organization. Rather than injuring society's sense of community, a robust individualism may indeed have enriched some communal bonds because they were then the product of informed individual choices, not externally imposed authority. Moreover, the new individualism was commendably democratic in nature. Across a large portion of the American social spectrum, the pursuit of self-fulfillment in some form was widely available. And as personal goal, it became a genuine though elusive possibility open on various terms to all citizens.

It is also plausible that discomfort on the part of some critics with the rise of self in the 1960s was the result of a historic tension between the American political economy and American consumer culture. The inherent conflict was outlined with some elegance by Peter Clecak:

> Since the principal aim of progress is steady economic growth, the inducement to defer gratification lessens . . . when the economy reaches a condition of peacetime affluence, as it did in the late fifties and early sixties. And the latent material and psychological hedonism observed by critics from Tocqueville to Tom Wolfe pushes toward the cultural surface. In such circumstances, expectations of all sorts soared: material and psychological, personal and social. (1983, p. 111)[14]

## LEISURE, CONSUMPTION, AND CLASS

In addition to a new assertion of individualism and an increasing concern for self-development, other societal factors reinforced the growing interest in the leisure enthusiasms which formed the core subjects of the special-interest magazines in the 1960s. Anyone, it seemed, could take up golf, boating, tennis, photography, even flying. "The 'social location' of the individual (his social class or other position) no longer determines his lifestyle or values," wrote Daniel Bell. "For a significant portion of the population, the relation of social position to cultural style—particularly if one thinks in gross dimensions such as working class, middle class, and upper class—no longer holds" (1970, pp. 19-20).[15]

For many Americans, their leisure accomplishments indeed came to define their social station. As the social theorist Pierre Bourdieu (1984) wrote, "Cultural consumption [is] predisposed, consciously and deliberately or not, to fulfill a social function of legitimating social differences" (p. 7). Such consumption, noted the anthropologists Mary Douglas and Baron Isherwood (1979, p. 60), could be viewed as a form of information exchange essential to the demarcation of social relationships. But one could perhaps raise one's social status by engaging in the right forms of leisure—by being, in effect, recreationally correct.[16] The result, according to observers such as the economist Tibor Scitovsky (1976, pp. 118-119), was a new and widespread "status consumption" by many Americans. The objective was elevated rank within society, and one of the certain means to succeed was to win acceptance within a certain social class or group through proficiency at a sport, game, or hobby (see also Lancaster, 1966, pp. 132-157).[17]

An important factor was the wide variety of possible avocational outlets. If one didn't like tennis, there was always golf. If skiing required too much athleticism or seemed too dangerous, perhaps photography as a hobby would be more appropriate. The multiplicity of participation and performance standards within each pastime was also a source of appeal. Some boating enthusiasts, for example, could devote themselves to the competitive rigors of sailboat racing, whereas others could find placid contentment in leisurely weekend cruises. A private pilot's license could be a passport either to long-distance travel adventures in the latest twin-engine technological marvel, or to the quiet, stay-at-home joys of antique aircraft restoration. One result of this diversity and variety was that full "status satisfaction" was within the reach of a large number of different individuals.

As in the case of individualism, the rise in leisure consumption had its critics. To those with elitist pretensions, it may have been distressing that the aristocratic image of avocations such as tennis, golf, or equestrian riding persisted long after the material conditions of access were no longer quite so exclusionary. Others perhaps were distressed by the fulfillment of the 1873 prognostication of the celebrated economist Alfred Marshall. "The official distinction between working men and gentlemen will disappear," Marshall predicted, "[when] every man is a gentleman" (1925, pp. 101-118).

In *Social Limits to Growth*, the economist Fred Hirsch (1976) wrote disapprovingly of what he regarded as a paradox of affluence. An influential critic on the Left, Hirsch explicated the paradox thusly: Why is economic advance so compelling a goal, even though it yields disappointing fruits when most, if not all of us, achieve it? In his view, American's "commodity fetishism" was in large measure the fault of the media, particularly magazines. "The life depicted in the glossy magazines clearly is attractive to many of us," he wrote. "The snag is that . . . private goods have a public context, in the broad environmental conditions of the use; a context that their private marketing does not take properly into account. What is then wrong in the industrial system is not the delivery but the order" (pp. 1, 109).

A curious blend of Puritanism and Marxism may in part explain the difficulty some academics had with the headlong rush to leisure in the 1960s. As the social historian Peter Stearns (1990) wrote:

> Leisure has not been propelled into a clear mark of worth. . . . This in part reflects the dominance of a work-oriented elite, including many articulate intellectuals. . . . We are still not sure that we are supposed to play. . . . Thus a host of European Marxists progressively dissect leisure interests as opiates, distracting the masses from examination of reality—meaning work and economic relationships. Ordinary men

clearly do not agree. They are playing . . . [and] creating a new reality. They have yet, however, to receive intellectual benediction. (p. 192)[18]

Large numbers of middle-class Americans in the 1960s nevertheless did seem to want to reinvent themselves. Most important, there is little evidence suggesting that, for most of the population, the impulse was in any sense either deeply political or genuinely separatist. Rather, it could perhaps best be viewed as a value shift toward an amplified, *personalized* version of affluence-enabled consumption and social mobility, largely driven by leisure interests. And it was this same impulse that insured the profits of the magazines that successfully focused on those interests.

# 5

# THE KNOWLEDGE IMPERATIVE

MAGAZINES HAVE TO MATCH THE PERCEPTIONS THEIR READERS
HAVE OF THEMSELVES AS THOROUGHLY UNIQUE INDIVIDUALS.
—JOHN O'TOOLE (PERSONAL INTERVIEW, 1992)

## THE NEED TO KNOW

The shift toward more individually defined values in the early 1960s can be seen as the culmination of 15 years of postwar changes in the affluence, class structure, the consumption ethos, education levels, residential patterns, and the leisure time enjoyed by American society. How this in turn translated into an ever-growing and increasingly passionate readership of leisure-activity special-interest magazines hinged, at least to some degree, on the confluence between many readers' deeper needs and the magazines' ability to fulfill them.[1]

At the same time, changes in the advertising business, reflective of the more individualistic values of the 1960s, also contributed to the magazines' success. "The new freedoms affected many of us," recalled John O'Toole, president of the American Association of Advertising Agencies and former chairman of Foote, Cone & Belding, a prominent advertising agency. "Art directors, for example, believed they had to dress funny to demonstrate they had talent, and it seemed like everyone was growing sideburns, buying a Ferrari, divorcing their wife, and moving in with their secretary in Soho." Before the 1960s, most consumer advertising was deliberately aimed at the largest possible mass audience, and so contained little intelligence and no humor. Then William Bernbach, the creative head of the Doyle Dane Bernbach agency and leader of the movement toward a degree of irreverence in advertising, launched the Volkswagen "Bug" and Avis rental car campaigns. "The Avis ads," said O'Toole, "the ones with the line, *We're number two, we try harder,* were truly revolutionary." One result of the revolution was that many important advertising agencies sought out the smaller accounts of special-interest advertisers, willingly trading less commission income for greater creative freedom (personal interview, January 7, 1992; see also O'Toole, 1985).

Perhaps the decline in traditional values in the 1960s meant that many Americans no longer felt satisfactorily defined by their work or community. The traditional symbols of status and success—having a good job, driving an expensive car, residing in a showy house, sending one's children to elite schools, holding a position of visible responsibility in a community civic organization, or perhaps being a deacon in a local church—were no longer enough. As a result, many sought a sense of needed social differentiation through their leisure activities. And the fact that the pastimes were usually both difficult to master and unconnected to further economic gain may in fact have imbued them with even greater status and made them more attractive.

Part of the explanation may also lie in the widespread rejection in the 1960s of passive, more collectivist social values in favor of all manner of private skill sets and avocations. To ski, drive a car, play golf or tennis, travel to exotic off-the-beaten-path destinations, operate a boat, or photograph well implied not that one was wealthy, but that one was uniquely competent and adept as an individual. Adeptness at such demanding and difficult skills was appealing precisely because it involved, in the view of one social theorist, "an act of deciphering, decoding, which presupposes practical or explicit mastery of the cipher or code" (Bourdieu, 1984, p. 2). As more and more people achieved prosperity, many Americans may have found that affluence, so long an almost-universal emblem of success, was not enough. They yearned for a sense of personal competence, and for many that came to mean "leisure competence" and skill in their recreational activities.[2]

Leisure-goods manufacturers and marketers had long known that, as one economist wrote, "positional goods attract an increasing proportion of family expenditure as family income rises" (Hirsch, 1976, p. 28).[3] The more discretionary personal income a person has, the greater his or her willingness to spend on unessential needs. For many newly affluent enthusiasts, the products and services that made possible their leisure pastimes took on increased personal importance, often becoming objects of "consuming passion." To the delight of the magazines' advertisers, it was also evident that the formidable price of many of the leisure products such as boats, cameras, or diving equipment was not a deterrent for the audiences of these publications. "We call those objects valuable," wrote the political economist Georg Simmel, "that resist our desire to possess them" (1978, p. 67). In fact, the purchase of high-quality goods may in some sense have been regarded as a protest against mass consumption, particularly when, as was often the case, the best products required a particular competence to use.

There was also an apparent class or status element in the equation, born of the postwar rise in affluence and social mobility. Studies revealed that, for many, an increase in personal income could not be equated with a rise in personal satisfaction. Happiness, some social observers concluded, appeared to depend far more on where an individual stood in relation to the Joneses than on his or her absolute standard of living (see Easterlin,1974, pp. 89-125; Scitovsky, 1976, p. 135). It seemed that what was important was one's perception of one's ranking in society—however that might be defined—rather than one's absolute income level. With the wide affluence, many Americans were faced with the need for new self-definitions. The central questions became: "Who am I? What is my status? How do I think others perceive me?"

Historically, certain ritualistic practices have been the province of a society's elite. In many primitive cultures, for example, symbolic individuals of the highest rank in the society often have performed rituals of gracious living as expressions of social and cultural superiority. In many cases, the elites' leisure observances not only served as public rituals for lower members of society to admire, but also helped underscore "ingroup" values that may have been threatened by outside forces. In more developed cultures, aristocracies have often defined themselves through their martial and leisure virtues, not by their economic attainments. What mattered was not the actual size of one's bank account, but the display and recognition of one's avocational accomplishments. The social importance, for instance, of "riding to the hounds," commanding the rank of Commodore at a local yacht club, or having a den displaying exotic trophies of the big-game hunter or sport fisherman, was not to be taken lightly. All were evidence of knowing how to "live well"—which, in turn, was one of the crucial markers of elevated social status.[4]

It was also important that many of the leisure pastimes contained their own cultural, symbolic, and historical associations. "The universe of sporting activities . . . presents itself to each new entrant as a set of ready-made . . . traditions, rules, values, equipment, and symbols," wrote the sociologist Pierre Bourdieu (1984), "which receive their social significance from the system they constitute and which derive a portion of their properties . . . from history" (p. 209). The arcane scoring practices of tennis, for example, illuminate Bourdieu's point. The game's traditional point enumerators—"love" (i.e. zero), "15," "30," and "40" leading to determinations of "game," "set," and "match"—were an essential part of an important ritual based on the historic origins of the sport. Similarly, a dictionary's worth of nautical terms, most derived from a long-past era of grand sailing ships, was eagerly learned by each new weekend boating enthusiast. To accept these rules and traditions, to display one's knowledge of them, was to certify one's standing as a bona fide participant in the sport.

It can be argued that certain leisure equipment itself had important class attributes. Such equipment not only formed the material basis for its owner's participation in a particular leisure activity, but was also encoded with social and rhetorical significance. As such, much equipment was clearly imbued with attributes of luxury and aristocracy. The anthropologist Arjun Appadurai (1986, p. 38) listed what he believed to be the critical requirements: complexity of acquisition, semiotic virtuosity, and specialized knowledge needed for appropriate use. Perhaps more important, one could draw some linkage between the product's use and the personality of its consumer. Owning the most technologically advanced skis, or the latest single-lens reflex camera for photography, not only suggested that the owners had the economic means to purchase the highest quality and most current equipment available, but their possession also demonstrated that they were knowledgeable, practiced, skilled, and perhaps even adventurous enough to use it.[5]

Surveying the variety of popular new forms of recreation, Pierre Bourdieu (1984) observed:

> How could one fail to recognize the dynamics of the dream of social weightlessness as the basis for all the new sporting activities—foot-trekking . . . canoeing, archery, windsurfing, cross-country skiing, sailing, hang-gliding . . . etc.—whose common feature is that they all demand a high investment of cultural capital in the activity itself, in preparing, maintaining, and using the equipment, and especially, perhaps, in verbalizing the experiences. (p. 220)

As it had throughout American history, education framed another dimension of class in the 1960s. "I thought of it as the 'Americanization of

America,'" recalled one magazine publisher. "The United States was a child of the Enlightenment, and the notions of progress and human perfectibility through education were always very important" (William Ziff, personal interview, February 8, 1991; March 5, 1991; March 12, 1991). Although graduation from an elite private secondary school, as it had since the late 19th century, continued to be a marker of upper-class status, the huge increases in postwar college enrollments soon resulted in unimagined social mobility for many Americans. The unique phenomenon of mass post-secondary education, however, meant not only social mobility, but also that many young people would find themselves in a social class different from their families'. For new first-generation graduates from the more elite colleges, life possibilities were expanded well beyond the social stations of their parents. As they entered adulthood, many would use their recreational interests—and their enthusiastic readership of magazines devoted to them—to confirm their new standing.[6]

At the same time, the rise in education levels itself was, in the view of publishing officials, clearly associated with increased magazine readership. "Education is the most important factor in magazine consumption," said Michael Hadley, former president of Times Mirror Magazines. "It equates to discretionary income, and therefore involvement in discretionary interests" (personal interview, December 23, 1991).[7] Many of the new college graduates were members of the postwar "baby-boom" generation, the birth cohort whose sensibilities came to define much of the postwar social ethos. To the delight of the publishing industry, they were in fact particularly avid readers of magazines. "Baby boomers were the pig in the python," recalled Gilbert Maurer of Hearst. "Both publishers and advertisers took it as an article of faith that they were our best customers, and created new magazines specifically aimed at their interests" (personal interview, December 23, 1991).[8]

The 1960s were certainly a time of pronounced individualism. Despite—as well as because of—this, a countervailing need was perhaps present. For many individuals, there may also have been a yearning for a sense of belongingness and community. For many people, self-fulfillment would always rely on various voluntary forms of association. No matter how important a sense of independence might be, personal fulfillment would, to some degree, always require close relations with others, as well as shared participation in shared cultural ceremonies and symbols. The rise of the suburbs, as well as the beginnings of change in patterns of family association and structure, contributed to a decline of both traditional neighborhoods and social rituals; the result was a widely felt loss of a sense of belonging. Many of the burgeoning leisure pursuits, however, clearly had strong communitarian aspects which may have formed the basis of some of their appeal. Pierre Bourdieu (1984) noted that sports such as tennis, golf, and yachting included an "obligatory manner of dress and behavior, and socializing techniques" (p. 217). The possibility of bonding with other like-minded individuals, forming or joining clubs in which to share and compare "grades of passionate judgment," participating in activity-based events, and taking tours organized around a particular avocation certainly must have been attractive (Douglas & Isherwood, 1979, p. 75).

For many enthusiasts, it is even possible that the activities themselves served as substitutes for a more conventional sense of community, replacements for the lost small-town sociality so central to the enduring American myth. In this context, the special-interest magazines may have served not only the small town's newspaper, but as both an essential element in the coherence and an important validator of these communities' very existence.

## THE SEARCH FOR THE RIGHT READER

The publishing companies' ability to produce successful magazines that would speak to these needs and desires centered in large part on accurately *segmenting* the potential audiences. It would not, for example, be enough simply to publish a magazine about flying in general; the publication would have to be about a particular collection of aspects of private aviation. Only then could a magazine publisher be confident that it would win and hold the loyalty of a definable group of readers, as well as be able to deliver a unified cluster of potential customers to prospective advertisers.[9]

The key to this process was known by a number of terms, but the most descriptive was "the analyzing variable." It would determine, within a given recreational field and with an eye toward existing competing publications, exactly what kind of magazine should be produced for exactly what segment of a potential audience. The analyzing variable would also help the publishers select the right editorial voice of a proposed magazine, as well as both the kind of topics it should cover and the manner in which they should be addressed. At the same time, it would define what the correct readership for that publication would be (Rankin, 1984).[10]

In the late 1950s, determining the analyzing variable for a given special-interest field was a largely intuitive process carried out by the senior executives at the publishing companies. More refined techniques of demographic and marketing analysis did not yet exist, and many of the deliberations were, by today's business standards, quite informal. In retrospect, however, the somewhat ad hoc nature of the decision-making process, did not seem to be a disadvantage. Indeed, more institutionalized efforts by publishers to create and test new magazine concepts, such as

Time, Inc.'s Magazine Development Group, that appeared in the late 1970s and early 1980s often produced less successful results.

A pair of actual examples from the late 1950s, one drawn from the world of boating magazines and one from the automotive field, can serve to illustrate the analytical process.

In early 1957, it seemed evident to at least one publisher of specialized publications, Ziff-Davis Publishing, that the boating arena was ripe for a new special-interest magazine. The two major existing titles, *Yachting* and *Motor Boating & Sailing*, had been in business for many years. It was apparent from analyses of their editorial content and their advertising, however, that both were positioned to appeal primarily to older, wealthier people. *Yachting*'s advertising sales materials, for example, made much of the claim that a large portion of the magazine's audience was the old-money owners of large sailboats, many of whom were members of the New York Yacht Club. Similarly, most of the editorial coverage in *Motor Boating & Sailing* was consciously aimed at the prosperous owners of large power cruisers. In the case of both publications, however, it can also be surmised that a portion of their readerships must have included less wealthy boating enthusiasts who enjoyed fantasizing about one day owning a large, luxurious sailing or motor yacht.

"But the United States was filling up with coastline. Those mighty beavers, the U.S. Army Corps of Engineers, were impounding every little stream in the country," remembered William Ziff, chairman of Ziff-Davis. Equally important, the 1950s were a time of great technological ferment in the boating world. Fiberglass construction techniques were perfected, and the new material would soon replace wood in most recreational boats. Marine engine technology matured, and outboard motors became much more reliable; as a result, the number of outboards in use increased from 2.8 million in 1950 to 5.8 million in 1960. In addition, new engine designs such as the inboard-outboard were winning widespread popularity. "Everything was happening," said William Ziff, "and there were all these people in a mad dash for the water" (personal interview, 1991; see also U.S. Department of Commerce, 1980, p. 206).

The problem, however, was that most of these new boating enthusiasts did not really need a boating magazine, new or otherwise. They might fish a little, dabble at water-skiing, perhaps just have a barbecue on the dock. As it turned out, the key to understanding what sort of person would require a new boating magazine, the analyzing variable, was that some of these people would be buying boats just big enough to leave sight of land or to overnight on. Their freshly bought toy could best be understood not as a boat, but rather as a quite dangerous seagoing house. New to the water and never members of a traditional yacht club, these novice yachtsmen and boating enthusiasts would have pressing informational

requirements which were not being met by the existing boating publications. Specifically, they would have an urgent and continuing need for
friendly reassurance and knowledgeable tutorials on seamanship, as well
as specific product information on such items as navigational instruments
and cabin furnishings (Furman Hebb, former executive vice-president, Ziff-
Davis Publishing, personal interview, February 1, 1991).

The result of these deliberations was launched in 1957 by Ziff-
Davis Publishing; its title was *Popular Boating* (the name was shortened to
*Boating* 10 years later). One of the most successful debuts in contemporary magazine history, its very first issue had a circulation of 100,000,
almost three times that of its older and more traditional competitors.
Within five years of its founding, *Boating's* monthly circulation had risen
to 188,000 and its annual advertising income was over $1 million. By the
end of the 1960s, its monthly circulation had passed 200,000, and its
annual advertising and circulation revenues were over $2 million (William
Phillips interview, March 15, 1991).

A similar success was enjoyed by a new automotive magazine
founded by Ziff-Davis in 1956 as *Sports Cars Illustrated* (its name was
changed in 1961 to *Car and Driver*). The mid-1950s were a time of hidden
ferment in the world of cars. "There were a growing cluster of people with
an active hatred for what Detroit was producing," William Ziff recalled.
Many were driving small European imports, but it was clear even in the
mid-1950s that, except for a quite small segment of luxury cars, the
European auto industry had entered a period of long, slow decline. More
important, however, these automotive enthusiasts were not part of the
conventional trade-up cycle; they were not simply buying a more luxurious version of what they already owned. This proved to be the analyzing
variable, because trade-up cycles can be viewed as learning curves. What
a person owns often determines what he will buy next. "What comes
next?" William Ziff asked. "Well, clearly it was going to be something
powerful, expensive, difficult to drive and difficult to maintain."

Though many of these people were driving underpowered
European sports cars, there seemed to be a clear appetite for improved
performance and better design. In the spirit of the times, more and more of
these individuals would want to be both fervent and finicky about their
cars. Automobiles would be not only a means of convenient travel, but, as
anthropological studies would later note, objects of passion, knowledgeable display, and connoisseurship. Many of these enthusiasts would also
attend motor races. Uninterested in basic transportation, they would want
to identify with automotive notions of mastery, danger, and technological
challenge.

And they would subscribe in large numbers to an automotive
enthusiasts' magazine that celebrated these same virtues. *Car and Driver*

was the product of these insights. By the mid-1960s, when Detroit began producing "performance cars" and the first products of Japanese engineering excellence began to arrive in America, it had become one of the dominant titles in the consumer automotive field. By the end of the decade, *Car and Driver's* monthly circulation was approaching 600,000, and its total advertising and circulation income was almost $3 million.

Using different analyzing variables to segment the automotive enthusiast audience, other magazine publishing companies were also able to introduce titles that soon found avid readerships. CBS's *Road & Track*, for example, created a narrow but profitable niche for itself by appealing to the elitist owners of inexpensive European sports cars; by the end of the 1960s, it had a monthly circulation just over 300,000. *Hot Rod*, a magazine published by Petersen Publishing, chose a broader editorial strategy by focusing on the specific informational needs of automotive "do-it-yourselfers" and hot-rodders, and its monthly circulation soon passed 800,000.[11]

By providing the right magazine for the right reader, parallel successes were enjoyed by magazine publishers in a number of special-interest fields in the 1960s. By the end of the decade, for example, both *Ski* and *Skiing* Magazines were able to take advantage of the widening interest in alpine skiing. The former had a monthly circulation of over 300,000; the latter, over 400,000. Similarly, both *Golf* and *Golf Digest* had monthly circulations approaching 500,000. And the hunting and fishing magazines, *Sports Afield*, *Field & Stream*, and *Outdoor Life*, all had more than 1 million monthly readers each.

In each case, these specialized magazines benefited from the burgeoning interest in specific avocations in the 1960s. By determining, albeit somewhat informally and intuitively, the important informational interests of a definable segment of each potential audience and then providing the specific kinds of editorial content designed to serve those interests, the magazines were able to succeed in both winning the loyalty of substantial and increasing numbers of active and committed readers and assembling an attractive, consuming audience that specific advertisers want to reach with their commercial appeals. And as a result, while their mass-market brethren were facing ever longer odds against their very survival, the special-interest magazine industry prospered.

# 6

# THE CALCULUS OF
# SUCCESS

I CONSIDER SUCH EASY VEHICLES OF KNOWLEDGE MORE HAP-
PILY CALCULATED THAN ANY OTHER TO STIMULATE . . . AN
ENLIGHTENED AND FREE PEOPLE.
   —GEORGE WASHINGTON (CITED IN RICHARDSON, 1931, P. 1)

## EDITORIAL PRIMACY

In virtually every instance, the success of the special-interest magazines in the 1960s was predicated on a collection of *editorial* principles and practices. In contrast to the ultimately self-defeating circulation machinations that the general-interest magazines used to compete with television for mass-market advertising dollars, the specialized magazines were editorially driven. Great attention was paid to editorial treatment and content, and much energy was focused on devising and refining editorial formulas which would appeal to their targeted audiences. As a result, the special-interest magazines were spared the difficulties that arose from management strategies designed to produce, not contented readers, but impressively large circulation totals to please mass advertisers (Bogart, 1956).[1]

Two key concepts were used to define the editorial character and positioning of special-interest magazines: *persona* and *structure*. One of the unique aspects of the magazine form itself was that most magazines possessed individual editorial personalities. Often termed the "editorial persona," it was the voice through which the publication spoke to its readers, and it set the tone for the entire editorial contents. Unlike that of a typical newspaper, the persona of a given magazine could almost be characterized as if it were a single individual. In most cases, this individual voice or persona also represented a set of values and attitudes with which the magazine's intended readership could be expected to sympathize. Most of the special-interest magazines sought to create distinct personas: clear, unmistakable, easily definable. Although in actual practice the nature of each publication's subject matter required subtle shadings and different emphases, the personalities of most specialized magazines shared a number of similar characteristics.

Perhaps the paramount quality was an essential enthusiasm on the part of the magazines for their subject matter. The readers had to feel that their devotion to and reverence for a specific avocation was reflected in the particular publication's point of view. In many instances, the readers had made large investments in money, time, and perhaps ego in the pursuit of their leisure activities, and the magazines' duty was to suggest ways to enhance their "return on investment," not to question the investment itself. Skiing enthusiasts, for example, looked to *Skiing* and *Ski* to reinforce their affection for the sport. Hobby pilots wanted *Flying* and *Pilot* to show them how to get more enjoyment out of their weekends aloft. At a time when Ralph Nader was pointing out the social costs of the automobile, enthusiasts expected a vigorous defense of the pleasures of car ownership from *Car and Driver*, *Road & Track*, and *Hot Rod*. Although there was a place for both occasional criticism and consideration of some of the possible dangers and costs involved, the specialized magazines all sought to reinforce rather than question their readers' chosen leisure interests.

Because one of the central motivations for readership was the audience's need for advice, assistance, and instruction, it was essential that the editorial persona of each special-interest magazine be an authority on the publication's subject. It had to be the voice of knowledge and experience. The knowledge, moreover, had to be of a practical, hands-on sort, with less immediate, more intellectual considerations kept to a minimum. Readers of *Popular Photography*, *American Photographer*, and *Petersen's Photographic* were less interested in theories of optics than in pragmatic advice on how to take better pictures. Hi-fi enthusiasts were eager to read in *Stereo Review* and *Audio* about the latest phonographic record releases and stereo equipment, not about the intricacies of electronic resistor theory.

Although the magazines' editorial personas represented an explicit and unequivocal source of reliable and expert authority, it was also important that they be able to offer their advice and recommendations in a benevolently tutorial manner. A certain sense of accessibility was crucial. Readers had to equate opening their magazines with entering a conversation with a knowledgeable and generous friend, eager to share wisdom and experience. The relative technical complexity of some of the special-interest avocations—the automotive, aviation, and boating fields, in particular—presented a unique editorial problem. In response, most of the magazines attempted to maintain a certain editorial balance. The preferred approach was to offer highly sophisticated treatments of complex subjects aimed at the expert enthusiasts who represented the publications' core readerships, while at the same time including a few articles that would meet the needs of entry-level readers. The goal, of course, was to assist in the education of the novices so that, through their loyal long-term readership of the magazines, they too would become—or, at a minimum, perhaps perceive themselves to be—experts.

In any consideration of a particular magazine's editorial persona, it is revealing to contrast it with an intuitive estimate of the characteristics of the publication's average reader. In virtually every instance, the persona of the magazine was slightly older, somewhat better educated and more affluent, more widely traveled, and certainly more worldly and sophisticated than the magazine's average reader. As a result, the editorial persona was ideally suited for the role of guide, counselor, friend, and adviser to the reader—which, in the case of most special-interest magazines, was the essence of its function.

The second major concept used to define the character of specialized magazines was their editorial structure (Janello & Jones, 1991, p. 7).[2] Because special-interest publications, like all magazines, were *periodicals*, they were faced with the need to "sell" themselves over and over again to the same audience of readers, both month after month at the newsstand and at subscription renewal time. Most publishers and editors believed that the most effective way to organize the editorial content of their magazines was a blend of the *expected* (that which would remain constant and could be looked forward to by the readers) and the *unexpected* (that which extended the readers' knowledge or exceeded their expectations).

In large measure, it was the editorial organization of the magazines—the major sectional elements used to segment the Table of Contents pages, as well as the recurring categories of stories within each section—that served as the constant for the readers. The actual articles themselves were the unexpected surprise. As a result, although there were new and different stories in each succeeding issue of any given magazine, the *kinds* of articles, reflective of the underlying editorial structure, varied very little (Lieberman, 1977).

Most of the special-interest magazines relied on three basic structural elements: columns, departments, and features. Columns, usually placed at the beginning of an issue, were used to represent a variety of viewpoints that the readers would find either instructive or entertaining. Rarely more than one typeset page (approximately 1,000 words) in length, columns were regarded as the appropriate vehicle for argument and opinion. Because of the personal nature of their perspectives, most columns were accompanied by a small photograph or illustration of their authors.

In most special-interest magazines, the first column in order of appearance was authored by the editor-in-chief, though it occasionally carried the publisher's byline. Often an editorial (in the newspaper sense) addressing a contemporary social, political, regulatory, or economic issue of concern to the magazine's readers, these editor's columns were usually given a title that suggested both the writer's authority and the particular leisure activity of the publication. Such columns in the automotive magazines, for example, were titled "Driver's Seat," "At the Wheel," and "On Track." In the magazines for boating enthusiasts, "At the Helm," "Crow's Nest," "Captain's Log," and "On Watch" were favored. The aviation publications used such headings as "From the Cockpit," "On Top," and "On Course." A few opted for simply "Editorial."

The editor's column was typically followed by three or four other columns, usually written by either senior editorial staff members or by contributing editors with long-term contracts with the publication. Though every magazine had its own mix of columnists, certain archetypes were often represented. One, for instance, might be the kindly, somewhat wistful voice of nostalgia, whose role was to explore the history and traditions of the sport. In contrast, another younger columnist might explore the challenges and excitement of the avocation's technological frontier. A third might be concerned with the formal competitive aspects of the sport: tournaments, regattas, races, and so forth.

A last, but certainly important category of columnist, was the celebrity figure. Often what that figure had to say may have been less important than the fact that he or she was saying it in the pages of the magazine. For the automotive or motorcycle magazines, the "star" columnist may have been a championship race driver or a prominent industry figure. For the boating publications, an America's Cup skipper or famous yacht designer would have similar appeal. Renowned test pilots and record holders commanded the right sort of reader respect in the aviation field. The golf and tennis magazines usually relied on the most celebrated professionals of the period. In most cases, the celebrity columnist's byline would appear over two kinds of columns. The first contained more general insights and opinions concerning "the state of the sport." The second, and more frequently employed, focused on helpful hints and tips on better technique and improved performance. In some cases, reader questions to the celebrity were encouraged, and the column then made possible a dialogue between The Star and Everyman.

Given the stringencies of space allotted to columns, as well as the nature of their typical subject matter, it was unusual for columns to be illustrated in any expansive way. In addition to a representation of the author at the top of the page, there was rarely space for anything more than a small identifying photograph or illustration, rarely larger than two inches by two inches.

The second major structural element utilized by special-interest magazines was departments. Positioned both in the front of the magazine after the columns and in the back of the publication, departments principally served a utilitarian function, providing "service" and "how-to" information. An important department in most magazines was the "Letters to the Editor" section, sometimes titled "Reader Forum," "Mailbag," or "Your Turn."

The Letters section was typically viewed as the proper vehicle for reader corrections, rebuttals, and disputes, and, as such, was considered an important reflection of reader involvement. Few specialized magazines responded in any great detail to the readers' comments, preferring to allow the readers to have the last word; the correspondence was, nevertheless, often edited for length and a minimum of style. In most cases, the magazines attempted to publish a variety of letters related to a range of previously published articles extending back three to six issues in the past. If, however, a particular article drew a notably large and volatile reader response, the entire Letters section would be devoted to that single subject.

Another category of department used by every special-interest magazine was the News section, in many instances titled "FYI" or "News Notes." Given the extended production lead times (often three months or more) under which most monthly magazines operated, the "news" supplied in these sections was often somewhat stale to any close follower of the subject. Because very little actual primary reporting was done, the principal sources for the information contained in most magazines' News sections were specialized industry publications, professional newsletters, and daily newspapers. Often a junior or mid-level editorial staffer would be assigned the responsibility of collecting these news items of possible interest to the magazine's readership. Once a month the staff member would assemble the items, rewriting them in summary form for inclusion in the News section. Although the information may not have been fresh by the time it reached the readers, it often was still news (Manousos interview, December 30, 1991).

New products were often the subject of another department. Major items of equipment were rarely treated in the New Product section, because the readers would expect a more comprehensive feature-length evaluation. As a result, the New Products department often focused on less important accessory and after-market items. With limited space to discuss each item and in the absence of any true evaluative effort, most New Product sections were purely descriptive. The source of the information on each product was usually limited to the material to be found in the manufacturer's press release. This information would often be hastily rewritten to serve as an extended caption to the accompanying photograph, also invariably supplied by the product's manufacturer or distributor.

Another popular department used the question-and-answer format to elicit and address reader concerns. Given the importance of equipment to most of the leisure activities covered by the special-interest magazines, many of these columns offered technical advice on maintenance and repair. In some magazines, this department took the form of sequential photographs intended to illustrate precisely how some complex task was to be performed. By following the instructional steps, the "do-it-yourself" reader could not only enjoy the satisfaction of a personal sense of independent competence but save money on maintenance and repairs as well (Menon, Bush, & Smart, 1987).

A few magazines, particularly those dealing with inherently dangerous avocations, devised departments that would use readers' "near-miss" experiences as a source of instruction for a wider audience. *Flying* had a department called "I Learned About Flying From That," whereas *Pilot* used a more ominous title, "Never Again." Similar departments were included in the special-interest magazines concerned with scuba diving and mountain climbing. The fundamental premise of such departments was that the lessons learned by a formerly errant, now chastened reader, would serve as a well regarded warning to fellow readers. In a sense, these departments may have served as both a welcome counterpoint to the unrelieved editorial authority of the publication's persona and a source of camaraderie among the readers.

In certain special-interest areas, organized competition was so fundamental to the readers' interests that it usually commanded feature treatment. Perhaps due to the emergence of televised professional tourneys, this was certainly the case with *Golf* and *Golf Digest*, and with *Tennis* and *World Tennis*. In other special-interest areas, however, the competitive aspects of the sport were viewed as less central to the readers' interests, and so coverage of competition was confined to a dedicated department, often placed in the rear of the publication.

A final departmental component used by virtually every specialized magazine was a calendar describing upcoming events and exhibitions.

Typically placed at the very end of the publication, these events calendars solicited listings from collectors groups, hobby associations, and sanctioning organizations. It was also hoped that the calendars would encourage participation at a local level and foster fellowship between like-minded enthusiasts, thereby increasing reader involvement in the avocation.

The third, and perhaps most important, structural element used by special-interest magazines was features. Though dependent on the overall size of a given issue, most magazines tried to include at least six features to accommodate a sense of overall editorial balance. As a rule, feature subjects lent themselves to longer (four or more pages) and more illustratively expansive treatment. The features were placed in what was termed the "feature well," after the columns and departments in the front of the magazine, and before the closing departments. With few exceptions, the first or "lead" feature was also the subject highlighted on that particular issue's cover. Additional features, however, were likely to be mentioned in secondary headlines (called "coverlines" or "cover blurbs") on the cover.

One notable aspect of features in special-interest magazines in the 1960s was the apparent waning interest in fiction. Although both the short story and longer fiction had long been a favored staple in magazines, by the late 1950s it was clear that they were falling from editorial favor. Throughout the 1960s, fewer and fewer magazines elected to publish fiction of any kind. A contributing factor may have been the postwar emergence of the paperback book industry, which made inexpensive fiction available to a wider reading audience. It is also possible that, with many Americans' appetite for pure entertainment being served by television, many magazine publishers believed that nonfictional forms of diversion would be the most secure franchise. And, indeed, some of the magazines that continued to feature fiction during the 1960s, such as the *Saturday Evening Post* and *True*, soon ceased publication. It would, however, be inaccurate to suggest that there was no place at all for fiction in the magazine form; although admittedly unique cases, both the *New Yorker* and *Reader's Digest* continue to include fiction features to this day (Janello & Jones, 1991, pp. 90-107; McFadden, 1983).[3]

Three fundamental themes were emphasized in the features in special-interest magazines: product evaluations, personal performance, "destination" articles. The magazine publishers took it as an article of faith that their readers' avocational interests revolved around a compelling need for product information. As a result, the magazines devised specific quantitative means to evaluate equipment. Some of the publications developed their own proprietary instrumentation with which to conduct the required tests, whereas other publishers contracted with private laboratories and testing facilities to provide the needed quantitative data.

Each issue included at least one, more often two, and sometimes three or more features writing up the results of those evaluations. In the automotive and motorcycle fields, the features were titled "road tests." The boating magazines called them "boat tests." In the aviation magazines, the results were termed "flight tests" or "pilot reports." The tennis, golf, photography and hi-fidelity publications referred to them as "lab reports" or "equipment tests." The format most often employed for these evaluations included a feature story of 2,500 to 3,500 words discussing in some detail the attributes of the product under consideration, a large number of photographs fully identifying the product (including, when applicable, interior details), and a "data panel" laying out in tabular form both the product's specifications and its performance results. Because these product evaluations both drew on and reinforced the inherent authority of the magazine as a whole, it was customary that they be published without the bylines of the editorial staffers who wrote the feature text or who conducted the evaluative tests.

An interesting variant on the basic product evaluation that often seemed to elicit enthusiastic reader reaction was the comparison test. Similar products that competed in a single market segment would be tested against each other, with a long list of attributes, features, and benefits compared. Some multiple tests examined only a pair of competitive products, whereas others would assemble a half dozen or more products for a larger and more extensive evaluation. In addition to the more obvious primary subjects such as cars, boats, planes, cameras, tennis racquets, and golf clubs, important accessories were also tested. Avionic equipment such as radios and radar, for instance, was a frequent comparison test subject in the aviation magazines, and the automotive and motorcycle publications often had extensive evaluations of high-performance tires.

The larger comparison tests would typically conclude with a rank ordering of all the products under consideration. The goal of the tests was to provide the readers with a knowledgeable opinion about the "best" individual item of equipment within the given product category. If one assumes that the subsequent Letters columns were a reasonable indicator, it is clear that the multiple-product evaluations were closely read. Perhaps motivated by simple brand loyalty, readers whose favorite products "lost" delighted in challenging the tests. Owners of the "winning" model or brand would, in contrast, express their approval of—indeed, thanks for— the positive evaluation.

The second major feature theme, improved or enhanced performance, was addressed in the special-interest magazines in a variety of ways. In each avocational subject area, a specific problem likely to confront many participants would be identified. Many tennis enthusiasts, for example, might want to improve their serve. Yachtsmen might benefit from advice on heavy-weather seamanship. Stereo speaker placement was an ongoing concern for audiophiles. Many camera buffs struggled with the intricacies of low-light photography. In each case, the enthusiasts could find the solution to their problems in the applicable special-interest magazine. Often cast as utilitarian "how-to" pieces and accompanied by explicit photographs or illustrations, many of the articles carried the bylines of prominent figures and well-known authorities in the sport, thus adding to the credibility of both the advice offered and the magazines themselves. And by adding to the readers' fund of knowledge about their chosen activity and making them more expert about its nuances, the publications both enhanced their readers' pleasure and rewarded them for their greater commitment to the pastime as a whole.

Stories focusing on interesting or exotic places in which to pursue one's chosen leisure activity were the third major feature theme developed in most special-interest magazines. Called "destination articles," they not only described the attractions of the location at great length (complete with attractive color photography), but also offered specific guidance on how to travel there, details of such matters as visa requirements and inoculations, and practical advice on what to pack. With the steady expansion during the 1960s of vacation travel, including trips to foreign locales, many Americans were willing to contemplate more distant holiday destinations. As a result, more resorts in both the continental United States and abroad began to offer activity-related vacation packages specifically designed for holiday sports enthusiasts. Among the foreign possibilities, the Caribbean and Mexico, with their easy proximity and friendly reputations regarding tourism, were the most popular destinations. The newly developed tennis resorts, golf camps, and scuba diving locales were widely covered in the tennis, golf, and diving magazines. Particularly during the winter months, most of the boating publications offered celebratory features describing the joys of yacht chartering in the islands, typically accompanied with lavish pictorials. Similarly, as the ski industry and its associated resort developments expanded in the American Rockies during the 1960s, the skiing magazines covered each new location in great and approving detail.

The editorial success of many of these destination articles, however, was clearly not dependent on the likelihood that every reader would have the money and time to use the information provided to actually take a trip. Rather, it is probable that, for a majority of the magazines' audiences, these articles offered only the raw material for fantasies and dreams. But for many readers, it seemed, being able to imagine themselves indulging in their favorite pastime in an exotic or glamorous locale was appealing enough.

## MANAGEMENT CONSIDERATIONS

The effective development of each special-interest magazine's editorial persona and structure was largely the responsibility of its editor-in-chief (often referred to as simply "the editor"). In addition to these conceptual tasks, the editor was also responsible for the management of the entire editorial operation. On most magazines, this included all of the editorial staffers, as well as the members of the publication's art department and freelance contributing writers, photographers, and illustrators. In most cases, both the editor and his counterpart in advertising sales, the advertising director, reported to the magazine's publisher. In small firms with only a single publication, both the circulation director and production director also reported to the publisher. The customary form of organization, however, at larger firms that published a number of magazines was based on a centralization of the circulation and production functions.

Editorial expenses typically represented approximately 10% of a magazine's total costs. (Advertising sales costs also accounted for 10% of the total expenditures, circulation represented 20%, and manufacturing/distribution consumed 50%; the remaining 10% was attributable to general administrative and overhead costs.) Within the editorial budget overseen by the editor, five major categories of expenditure were represented. Salaries and benefits for full time staff members typically accounted for 50%. The second largest item, often called "manuscripts and illustrations," was used to pay freelance writers, photographers, and illustrators; it frequently totaled 20% of the editorial budget. Three additional categories—costs associated with editorial travel and entertainment, office operations such as supplies and telephone charges, and special graphic and photography preparation expenses—each accounted for 10% (William Phillips interview, March 15, 1991).

As these numbers suggest, the area of greatest concern to most editors was the "salaries and benefits" category. The human resources available were, as in other knowledge-based enterprises, far more critical than the typewriters or telephones. "The only real assets any magazine publisher ever has," said William Ziff, chairman of Ziff-Davis Publishing, "walk out of the building every evening." The issue facing most special-interest magazine editors had both a quantitative and a qualitative dimension. As a rule of thumb for monthly publications, the customary staffing formula called for one full-time editorial employee for every seven pages of editorial matter in the issue. Prosperous, well-established magazines might employ a few more staffers than the formula suggests, and a struggling publication might make do with a few less.

More important than the number of people, however, was their "quality," specifically, the subject-area knowledge and expertise they could bring to bear on their writing and editing tasks. Most of the specialized publishers assumed that one could teach an automotive engineer, accomplished photographer, or experienced pilot the necessary journalistic skills of writing and editing. In contrast, they believed it far more difficult to hire "general-purpose" journalists with no strong personal interest or individual experience in the avocation, and then instruct them in the history, traditions, social attitudes, shared values, and skills required by the particular sport. This hiring practice had a number of effects. Often unschooled in the traditional tenets of conventional journalism, many special-interest magazine staffers found it difficult to set aside what might be termed a "fan mentality." It can be argued that this predisposed many of them to a less critical view of their subject matter. In some cases, after writing a sufficient volume of pleading letters, particularly avid readers were, in fact, hired to join the editorial staffs (Stanley R. Greenfield interview, December 19, 1991).

Due in large measure to the technical complexity of the subject matter covered by the special-interest magazines, most of the articles were written by full-time staff members. It was, however, important for each magazine to develop a trusted stable of regular freelance contributors. Typically paid between 5 and 50 cents per word for their efforts, these contributors were not only cost-effective sources of editorial copy, but also useful originators of fresh story ideas.

Despite the centrality of the editorial department to magazine publishing, from a management perspective it was correctly regarded as a "cost item." The two principal revenue sources were the key departments on the business side of publishing, circulation, and advertising. The main function of the circulation department was to sell the magazine to its readers, either as buyers of single copies on the newsstand or as subscribers. The primary task of the advertising department was to sell advertising space to manufacturers and distributors wishing to promote their goods and services to the readers of the publication.

Subscriptions typically represented 75% of the circulation of most special-interest magazines; the remaining 25% were single-copy sales. The least expensive source of subscribers was often orders from newsstand readers who returned the postage-paid card or order form included in the publication. Not only did such subscriptions cost comparatively little to obtain, but they also tended to renew at a higher rate once the original subscription had expired. To promote their magazines to new readers, many publishers also purchased lists of names and addresses. Perhaps the most productive sources for such lists were those assembled by manufacturers from product warranty cards. Other names and addresses were obtained from owners' groups, tour operators, and companies that specialized in brokering such lists. Promotional mailings would then be sent to these prospective subscribers offering them a subscription to the magazine, often at a discounted rate. Incentive premiums such as travel bags, coffee mugs, or items of apparel were often included to appeal to new subscribers.[4]

Most of the advertising space in special-interest magazines was bought by manufacturers and distributors of "generic" products directly related to the publications' areas of interest. Calculated on the customary basis of cost per thousand, the specialized magazines typically charged higher advertising rates than either general-interest publications, television, or radio. The advertisers, however, realized that their ads would be viewed by a concentrated group of potential customers, and therefore regarded the special-interest magazines as a good buy. In an effort to appeal to advertisers of "nongeneric" products such as tobacco and liquor, some publishing firms with a number of magazines offered a substantial discount if an advertiser placed an advertisement in all of the company's publications at the same time (Compaine, 1982, pp. 55-75).

At first glance, it appeared that the goals of the circulation and advertising departments were mutually supporting. One might expect, for example, that Circulation would attempt to sell the publication to as many readers as possible. And because the advertising rates were based on the number of readers reached, the more circulation a magazine had, the more it could charge for advertising. Following this logic, one might presume that Advertising delighted in ever-increasing circulation figures. In actual business practice, however, neither of these assumptions was completely true. To maximize revenues, most special-interest magazine companies developed management norms predicated on intrinsically conflicting objectives for their circulation and advertising efforts. Circulation was responsible for the publication's operating profitability, and Advertising was encouraged to be more concerned with competitive marketplace considerations (Rankin, 1984, pp. 216-229).[5]

As a result, the goal of most circulation departments was not simply to find more readers for their publications. Rather, their core responsibility was to optimize per-issue profit, while ensuring that the magazine was read by the number of readers that the advertisers had been promised would see their ads. Achieving this precise circulation goal was called "meeting the guaranteed rate base." As a matter of trade practice, this guaranteed number of readers was affirmed by the publication only once a year, at the time when its advertising rate structure was published as a matter of commercial record in a document called the rate card. The actual circulation was later confirmed by an independent auditing agency, the Audit Bureau of Circulation, by averaging the actual figures over subsequent 6- and 12-month periods.[6]

In the view of most circulation directors, the key to optimal circulation profitability lay in fine tuning the number of readers over the course of the year so that the audited circulation proved to be exactly at, or just above, the previously guaranteed rate base. This was accomplished by balancing reader demand with both the subscription and newsstand prices. If a publication, for example, suddenly became more popular, the circulation department would raise the subscription and cover price to absorb the new demand. As a result, revenues were increased without added manufacturing costs, thereby improving profitability. Equally important in the profit-oriented view of Circulation, the advertisers had only paid to reach the exact number of readers promised on the rate card. If a magazine's circulation were allowed to rise indiscriminately, advertisers would be given readers they had not "paid for." To prevent this, the circulation department attempted to manage rising reader demand to yield increased profit, until the next annual rate card change could reflect increased advertising rates.

In contrast to that of Circulation, the ethos in the Advertising departments of most special-interest magazines centered not on difficult calculations of profitability, but on the straightforward and tangible objective of increasing the total number of advertising pages sold. Salespersons' compensation, for example, was chiefly determined by page totals, and the management focus in advertising sales was largely concentrated on simple numerical improvement.

Arising from their differing perspectives, there were at least two common instances in which the interests of Advertising and Circulation diverged. To sell more ad pages, aggressive advertising departments looked for ways to offer prospective clients comparative price advantages. The most commonly used device was "bonus circulation." If the circulation was allowed to rise above that stipulated on the rate card, advertisers would be given "extra" readers, which would in effect lower the cost per thousand rate the advertiser was being charged. The same reason that made this strategy attractive to Advertising—the fact that advertisers were being given "free" readers—made it an anathema to the circulation department. A related issue of contention between the advertising and circulation departments involved the annual rate-card revisions driven by normal circulation growth. Because most specialized publications usually held their cost per thousand rates constant during such adjustments, the result was often an increase in the magazine's absolute advertising rates. Most sales departments feared that any demand for additional dollars from their advertisers would result in fewer ad pages sold.

Despite their conflicting goals and objectives, in most cases the special-interest magazines' circulation and advertising departments both made substantial contributions to their companies' income statements.

Because senior management, moreover, realized that a wise balancing of each departments' claims was essential to long-term economic success, neither side was ever permitted an absolute victory.[7]

A similar inherent tension often existed—indeed, was encouraged—between the editorial and advertising departments. An absolute "church and state" division between a magazine's journalistic and business efforts was not the norm in special-interest publishing. Few editors of specialized magazines had the power to insist on the kind of journalistic purity and business noninterference enjoyed by their colleagues on newspapers or the news magazines. The principal point of conflict between Editorial and Advertising usually involved the product evaluations. Most editors were aware that a negative review of a product manufactured by a major advertiser might result in a canceled advertising contract, and some may have exercised a certain editorial caution. When tens of thousands of dollars were at stake, often the mere threat of reprisal was enough to cause some editors second thoughts. In a few cases, smaller publications with weak managements were rumored to have allowed important advertisers to review evaluations prior to publication. To the credit of the majority of special-interest magazines, however, there is no evidence to suggest that such lapses of integrity were the industry norm. And, indeed, many of the specialized publications did in fact suffer the loss of advertising from time to time as a result of their efforts to provide their readers with honest product evaluations (Farley interview, December 23, 1991; Kummerfeld interview, December 23, 1991).[8]

A related issue concerned the influence of Advertising on the selection of products to be covered by Editorial. Although most editors sought to maintain a balance of subject matter to meet their readers needs, large advertisers would occasionally lobby for extensive coverage of their own products. In some instances, advertising salespeople would attempt to curry favor with their clients by trying to influence editorial decision making in such matters.

The best defense for any special-interest magazine editor faced with these or similar pressures was to restate the importance of keeping faith with one's readers. Every publication's editorial credibility rested on its readers' continued belief that the magazine shared not only their enthusiasm for the avocation, but also their sincere belief both in its intrinsic importance and its role in a life well lived.

To many of the more thoughtful observers of the publishing industry, it was clear that the long-term prospects of every specialized magazine hinged on this sense of shared values. And as more and more Americans during the 1960s came to possess the wherewithal and the inclination to pursue the leisure activities the publications celebrated, both the economic future of the special-interest magazines and their unique place in the lives of their readers was assured.

# 7

# CONCLUSION

PERHAPS THE MOST SIGNIFICANT REASON FOR THE MAGAZINE'S
SURVIVAL HAS BEEN ITS ABILITY TO ADAPT TO A CHANGING
ROLE IN SOCIETY.
—BENJAMIN M. COMPAINE (1990, P. 100)

## INTERNAL FACTORS

S uccess in any commercial publishing enterprise must certainly lie
both in the intellectual accuracy of original design and in the details
of operational execution. It is clear, however, that in the 1960s the
American consumer magazine industry as a whole underwent a profound
transformation which can be characterized by two central trends: the
decline of many large mass-market, general-interest publications, and the
emergence of a wide variety of smaller, special-interest magazines focused
on specific leisure and recreational subjects and aimed at specialized
audiences.

There is ample evidence to suggest that this transformation was driven, in part, by internal economic factors within the magazine publishing industry. Beginning in the late 1950s, television posed a growing threat to the general-interest magazines' principal source of revenue: the advertising income earned from national manufacturers of mass-market products and services. By the mid-1960s, it was apparent to many observers that the mass magazines possessed few, if any, comparative advantages in their competition with television for national advertising dollars. Many mass magazines remained wedded, nevertheless, to expansive circulation strategies which they hoped would continue to justify ever-increasing advertising rates. This proved to be a serious management miscalculation. During the 1960s, the costs associated with maintaining the mass magazines' large circulations mounted and the total number of advertising pages declined. By the early 1970s, many of the publications had been forced to cease publication.

Although these internal factors made profitable mass-magazine publishing an increasingly problematic proposition, other industry changes in the 1960s favored the rise of smaller, more specialized publications. Major advances in printing technology not only lowered costs but changed the economies of scale in magazine publishing. The development of compact, high-quality offset presses, as well as the computerization of typesetting and color-separation processes, resulted in reduced per-copy manufacturing costs. Large print runs lost their economic advantage, and small circulation magazines became more profitable. Even more important was the advent in the early 1960s of a philosophy of "targeted" marketing by major consumer-goods manufacturers. As computer technology evolved and its commercial use became more widespread, many marketers recognized the efficiency of aiming their advertising at narrowly defined segments of potential customers. The result was a marketing revolution; for those advertisers who understood the new approach, finding the largest possible audience was no longer the unchallenged goal.

One of the fundamental premises of special-interest magazine publishing was uniquely suited to this new view of marketing. Through their choices of editorial subjects and treatments, the publishing companies consciously worked to target their specialized magazines at definable groups of readers. An important by-product of this effort was that they were then able to deliver a unified cluster of potential customers to prospective advertisers. With their smaller, more homogeneous readerships, the rise of targeted marketing clearly favored the special-interest magazines as advertising media. Particularly attractive was the fact that many of the specialized magazines were read by a disproportionate number of upscale males, a market segment that national advertisers had traditionally found difficult to reach. Given their evident efficiency as advertising vehicles, the magazines were able to raise dramatically their advertising rates, in some cases more than tripling them during the course of the decade. As a result, publishers who concentrated their efforts on specialized magazines in the 1960s enjoyed significant advantages in both circulation and advertising income.

## PRODUCT AND CATALYST

Internal economic considerations, however, may not be a complete explanation for the transformation of the magazine industry. It also can be argued that the decline of large mass-market, general-interest publications and the rise of smaller, special-interest magazines during the 1960s were evidence of more general, and more profound, sociocultural changes in American society. Like all communications media, magazines are not merely self-contained journalistic or economic artifacts. In a larger context, they can also be interpreted as both products and catalysts of the social and cultural realities of their time. They can serve as windows into the tenor, spirit, attitudes, concerns, and underlying values of their age. And they help shape those very attitudes and values.

In this view, the mass-audience, general-interest magazines of the 1950s such as *Life, Look,* and the *Saturday Evening Post* reflected and reinforced the broad consensus and conformist ideology of the first 15 years following World War II. For the first time in any nation's history, a large majority of citizens was economically enfranchised. Propelled by the postwar rise in affluence, education and suburbanization, the mass magazines both mirrored and advanced traditional middle-class notions of "the good life."

With the arrival of the 1960s, the essential social consensus and cultural coherence of American society that so characterized the previous decade and a half began to fractionate. Conventional interpretations of the 1960s have long centered on the widespread protest against the prevailing social and political norms. It is also possible, however, that America underwent a concurrent, perhaps even broader based, social change in the 1960s. Less concerned with contemporary aspirations for political and social justice, it was animated instead by an ardent desire for *personal* fulfillment, defined by new notions of identity and individualism, class and community, and leisure consumption and competence. This little noticed but significant value shift, well before both the "Me Decade" of the 1970s and the "Gimme Decade" of the 1980s, might be called "The Other 1960s." A major value reorientation in American life, it both provided the societal context from which modern special-interest magazines arose and was significantly furthered by their success.

For the millions of readers of successful special-interest magazines in the 1960s, the quest of the age may not have been for social justice or political reform, but rather for new expressions of individuality and new outlets for personal self-fulfillment. Empowered with affluence and education, happy to be enlisted in an ascending social class, free of the conformist strictures of the 1950s, but cut off from traditional communal sources of identity and social status, many turned to active leisure pursuits to add coherence and meaning to their lives.

It is always difficult to judge the meaning to be found in another person's life, let alone that of a nation. But with every magazine subscription order and newsstand purchase, clearly the dreams of many Americans in the 1960s provided both the larger societal context and the entrepreneurial rewards that insured the triumph of the American special-interest magazine.

# APPENDIX: TABLES

TABLE 1. U.S. CONSUMER MAGAZINE SUBSCRIPTION AND SINGLE-COPY CIRCULATION, 1955-1970.

| Year | Subscription Circulation (percent) | Single-Copy Circulation (percent) |
|---|---|---|
| 1955 | 60.5 | 39.5 |
| 1960 | 67.3 | 32.7 |
| 1965 | 69.1 | 30.9 |
| 1970 | 71.0 | 29.0 |
| Relative percentage increase (decrease): | | |
| 1955-1960 | 11.2 | (17.2%) |
| 1960-1965 | 2.7 | (5.5) |
| 1965-1970 | 2.7 | (6.1) |

Source: Compaine, B.M. (1982). *The Business of Consumer Magazines*, p. 24. (White Plains, NY: Knowledge Industry Publications).

*Discussion:* Despite the importance placed by some publishers on single-copy sales as an indicator of editorial "vitality," it is clear that the general trend of the period favored the growth of subscription circulation. The rise of the suburbs and a decrease in the number of urban newsstands certainly played a role in this shift in magazine circulation patterns.

### TABLE 2. U.S. CONSUMER MAGAZINE CIRCULATION, 1960-1970.

| Year | Number of ABC-Audited Magazines | Aggregate Circulation Per Issue (millions) | Average Circulation Per Issue (thousands) |
|------|------|------|------|
| 1960 | 545 | 245.0 | 450 |
| 1965 | 768 | 291.9 | 380 |
| 1970 | 1009 | 307.0 | 304 |
| Percentage increase (decrease): | | | |
| 1960-1965 | 40.7 | 19.1 | (15.6) |
| 1965-1970 | 31.4 | 5.2 | (20.0) |

Source: Compaine, B.M. (1982). *The Business of Consumer Magazines*, p. 9. (White Plains, NY: Knowledge Industry Publications).

*Discussion:* The 1960s were a time of magazine proliferation. Although both the number of Audit Bureau of Circulation-audited consumer magazines and their aggregate circulations increased, the average circulation size of magazines fell from 450,000 readers per issue to 304,000, a decrease over the decade of more than 30%. More magazines were being published, but they were aimed at smaller audiences.

## TABLE 3. U.S. PERIODICAL PUBLISHING, 1950-1970.

| Year | Number of Periodicals | Personal Expenditures on Periodicals (billions) |
|---|---|---|
| 1950 | 6960 | 1.49 |
| 1960 | 8422 | 2.19 |
| 1970 | 9573 | 3.90 |
| Percentage increase: | | |
| 1950-1960 | 21.0 | 47.0 |
| 1960-1970 | 13.7 | 78.1 |

Sources: U.S. Department of Commerce, Bureau of the Census. (1975). Historical Statistics of the United States: Colonial Times to 1970. Washington, DC: U.S. Government Printing Office; U.S. Department of Commerce, Bureau of the Census. (1950-1980). Statistical Abstract of the United States. Washington, DC: U.S. Government Printing Office.

## TABLE 4. COMPARISON OF GNP TO VALUE OF PERIODICAL INDUSTRY SHIPMENTS, 1960-1975.

| Year | U.S. GNP (billions) | Industry Value (billions) | Industry Portion of GNP (percent) |
|---|---|---|---|
| 1960 | 506.0 | 2.1 | 0.0041 |
| 1965 | 688.1 | 2.6 | 0.0038 |
| 1970 | 982.4 | 3.2 | 0.0033 |
| 1975 | 1528.8 | 4.4 | 0.0029 |

Sources: U.S. Department of Commerce, Bureau of Economic Analysis. (1965, 1971, 1976). U.S. Industrial Outlook. Washington, DC: U.S. Government Printing Office.

TABLE 5. U.S. PERIODICAL PUBLISHING INDUSTRY, 1958-1977.

| Year | Number of Companies | Industry Value (billions) | Value Share of 8 Largest Companies (percent) |
|------|--------------------|-----------------------|------------------------------------|
| 1958 | 2246 | 1.7 | 41 |
| 1967 | 2430 | 3.1 | 37 |
| 1977 | 2860 | 6.1 | 35 |

Source: U.S. Department of Commerce, Bureau of the Census. (1977). Census of Manufacturers. Washington, DC: U.S. Government Printing Office.

*Discussion:* Between 1950 and 1970, the U.S. periodical industry as a whole prospered. The total number of periodicals increased by more than a third, and personal expenditures for periodicals more than doubled (see Table 3). But despite the periodical industry's growth during the 1960s and early 1970s, its relative share of the GNP declined (see Table 4). And as the number of publishing companies and their revenues increased, industry concentration decreased slightly (see Table 5).

TABLE 6. MAGAZINE READERSHIP BY AGE, 1957-1976.

| Age | 1957 Survey (percent)[a] | 1966 Survey (percent) | 1976 Survey percent) |
|-----|------------------------|----------------------|---------------------|
| 20-29 | 29 | 24 | 30 |
| 30-39 | 25 | 21 | 28 |
| 40-49 | 25 | 22 | 24 |
| 50-59 | 25 | 27 | 26 |
| 60+ | 27 | 27 | 27 |
| Overall | 27 | 25 | 28 |

[a]Percentage of respondents to national surveys indicating that they read a magazine "yesterday."
Source: Robinson, J.P. (1980, Winter).The changing reading habits of the American public. *Journal of Communication, 30*(1), p. 147.

*Discussion:* It is apparent that the advent of television had no lasting effect on the appeal of magazines. Despite a small decline in overall magazine readership in the 1960s, by the mid-1970s it had surpassed the level it had attained prior to the dominance of television. Perhaps largely due to a proliferation of special-interest titles, magazines also regained the loyalty of younger readers.

TABLE 7. COMPARISON OF LEISURE ACTIVITIES AND MAGAZINE READERSHIP.

| Activity | Total Sample (percent) | Read Magazines (percent) | Read Books & Magazines (percent) |
|---|---|---|---|
| Gardening | 41 | 38 | 43 |
| Outdoors activities (e.g. camping) | 35 | 32 | 38 |
| Individual sports (e.g. golf) | 33 | 24 | 42 |
| Physical fitness (e.g bicycling) | 33 | 24 | 39 |

Source: McEvoy, G.F., & Vincent, C.S. (1980, Winter). Who reads and why? *Journal of Communication, 30*(1), p. 138.

*Discussion:* The fear on the part of some industry observers that an increased interest in recreation might lower Americans' appetite for reading proved unfounded. Indeed, for magazine publishers, there was a reassuringly high correlation between the pursuit of leisure activities and magazine readership.

TABLE 8. BOATING MAGAZINE, ECONOMIC DATA, 1963-1970.

|  | 1963 | 1966 | 1970 |
|---|---|---|---|
| Total Advertising Pages | 720 | 680 | 963 |
| Page Rate, 1xB&W ($) | 1695 | 1780 | 2010 |
| Circulation (000s) | 188 | 193 | 204 |
| Operating Statements ($000): |  |  |  |
| Advertising Income | 1051 | 1084 | 1643 |
| Circulation Income | 347 | 393 | 573 |
| Subscription Income | 198 | 227 | 359 |
| Single-copy Income | 149 | 166 | 214 |
| Other Income | 0 | 0 | 20 |
| Total Income | 1398 | 1484 | 2236 |
| Operating Profit | 152 | 126 | 435 |

Source: William Phillips (treasurer, Ziff Communications, interview by author, March 15, 1991, New York.

TABLE 9. CAR AND DRIVER MAGAZINE, ECONOMIC DATA, 1963-1970.

|  | 1963 | 1966 | 1970 |
|---|---|---|---|
| Total Advertising Pages | 398 | 477 | 533 |
| Page Rate, 1xB&W ($) | 1585 | 3150 | 6215 |
| Circulation (000s) | 228 | 303 | 577 |
| Operating Statements ($000): |  |  |  |
| Advertising Income | 817 | 1295 | 1947 |
| Circulation Income | 665 | 967 | 1238 |
| Subscription Income | 379 | 546 | 885 |
| Single-copy Income | 286 | 421 | 353 |
| Other Income | 0 | 61 | 38 |
| Total Income | 1482 | 2323 | 3223 |
| Operating Profit | 325 | 677 | 835 |

Source: William Phillips (treasurer, Ziff Communications), interview by author, March 15, 1991, New York.

TABLE 10. FLYING MAGAZINE, ECONOMIC DATA, 1963-1970.

|  | 1963 | 1966 | 1970 |
|---|---|---|---|
| Total Advertising Pages | 570 | 780 | 705 |
| Page Rate, 1xB&W ($) | 1755 | 2299 | 3655 |
| Circulation (000s) | 220 | 257 | 347 |
| Operating Statements ($000): |  |  |  |
| Advertising Income | 1051 | 1084 | 1643 |
| Circulation Income | 347 | 393 | 573 |
|    Subscription Income | 198 | 227 | 359 |
|    Single-copy Income | 149 | 166 | 214 |
| Other Income | 0 | 0 | 20 |
| Total Income | 1398 | 1484 | 2236 |
| Operating Profit | 152 | 126 | 435 |

Source: William Phillips (treasurer, Ziff Communications, interview by author, March 15, 1991, New York.

TABLE 11. POPULAR PHOTOGRAPHY MAGAZINE, ECONOMIC DATA, 1963-1970.

|  | 1963 | 1966 | 1970 |
|---|---|---|---|
| Total Advertising Pages | 907 | 1103 | 1200 |
| Page Rate, 1xB&W ($) | 3853 | 4315 | 6797 |
| Circulation (000s) | 397 | 417 | 535 |
| Operating Statements ($000): |  |  |  |
| Advertising Income | 1888 | 2456 | 3647 |
| Circulation Income | 925 | 1040 | 1276 |
|    Subscription Income | 473 | 554 | 637 |
|    Single-copy Income | 452 | 486 | 639 |
| Other Income | 0 | 7 | 75 |
| Total Income | 2813 | 3503 | 4998 |
| Operating Profit | 496 | 843 | 1506 |

Source: William Phillips (treasurer, Ziff Communications, interview by author, March 15, 1991, New York.

*Discussion:* A review of historical economic data from four representative special-interest magazines suggests the bases of their financial success during the 1960s. *Boating* (Table 8), *Car and Driver* (Table 9), *Flying,* (Table 10), and *Popular Photography* (Table 11), all enjoyed increases in total advertising pages sold, the rates charged for advertising, and total circulation. As a result, revenues from both advertising and circulation increased, yielding significant profit growth.

As noted in the text, the attractiveness to potential advertisers of the audiences of the special-interest magazines allowed the magazines to effect substantial annual increases in their advertising rates. Due to this evident "elasticity" in advertising rates, advertising revenues typically represented a larger share of total income than circulation revenues.

# NOTES

## CHAPTER 1

1. A national poll in late September 1960 revealed that 62% of the
   adult U.S. population had watched or listened to the debate. Of
   those who had, 23% thought Nixon "did a better job," 29% rated it a
   tie, and 44% favored Kennedy's performance (see Gallup, 1960).
   Note: The Gallup poll combined the TV and radio audiences; however, to some radio listeners, Kennedy's victory may have been less
   obvious.
2. See *Life* (1960, October 10, pp. 30, 150-157); *Look* (1960, October
   11, pp. 93-99).
3. Introduced in 1947, commercial television's advertising revenues
   had first surpassed those of magazines in 1954, but the late 1950s
   saw little relative change. In 1961, however, magazine ad revenues
   experienced a small decline, whereas TV revenues increased dramatically. By 1963, television's ad income was double that of magazines. See van Zuilen (1977, pp. 166-167); see also Compaine
   (1974).
4. *The Saturday Evening Post* folded in 1969, *Look* in 1971, and the
   original weekly *Life* in 1972. *Collier's,* once a significant mass-circulation rival, had ceased publication in 1956, but its demise was

largely unrelated to television. See Alpert (1957, pp. 9-11); see also Friedrich (1970), Wood (1971), Kobler (1968), White (1968), and Elson, Prendergast, and Colvin (1986).

5. For a provocative analysis of the economic determinants that are often unconsidered in popular culture studies, see Nord (1980, pp. 17-31). Epstein (1974) and Bagdikian (1987) are two of the more useful works of structural media criticism.

6. A good summary of the class assumptions of the 1950s prosperity can be found in Lears (1989, pp. 38-57).

7. For an insightful discussion of the prevailing notions of privacy, see also Jackson (1985, p. 281).

8. Between 1964 and 1983, 116 of 1,917 articles published concerned magazines; 53% were content analyses, 22% were historical in nature, and 11% dealt with economics. See Gerlach (1987, pp. 178-182); see also Jacobson (1988, pp. 511-514).

9. *Communication Abstracts* from 1978 (its first year of publication) to 1991 were analyzed by the author, using the index headings of *Magazine, Magazine Readership*, and *Magazine History* (but not *Magazine Advertising*). Magazine research represented 151 and 15,900 articles (0.95%) and averaged just under 11 articles per annual volume. Newspaper research averaged over 60 articles per issue; television over 200.

10. The two most widely cited works of magazine history are Mott (1938) and Peterson (1956). Other narrative histories include Richardson (1931), Wolseley (1951), Davenport and Derieux (1960), Ford (1969), Tebbel (1969), Wood (1971), Taft (1982) Tebbel and Zuckerman (1991), and Janello and Jones (1991). Though newspapers rather than magazines are its principal focus, see also Emery and Emery (1991).

11. For other early scholarship on media development, see DeFleur (1970), Lasswell (1972), and Gordon (1975, 1977).

12. For a further consideration of the magazine life stages, see also Felker (1969, p. 7), and Koback (1972, p. 45).


## CHAPTER 2


1. Although two other mass-audience magazines, *Reader's Digest* (12.1 million) and *TV Guide* (7.0 million), would by 1960 surpass the circulations of *Life* (6.1 million), the *Saturday Evening Post* (6.0), and *Look* (5.7 million), it can be argued that the centrality of the "Big Three" to the postwar cultural ethos, as well as their larger physical size, justified the label of "flagship." For historical circulation data, see Damon-Moore (1987, pp. 19-21). Note: The provenance of this Alfred Eisenstaedt photo, particularly the question of its spontaneity, has long been a subject of speculation which the accompanying text

did little to dispel. In a style often favored by *Life*, it read: "New photographers had long trained servicemen to assume ardent poses for the camera, but there was little posing in last week's coast-to-coast kissing." As some have pointed out, "little" does not mean "no." See "Victory Celebrations," *Life* (1945, August 27, pp. 26-27).

2.  For a thoughtful study of the role of the Depression in postwar attitudes, see Elder (1974); see also Easterlin (1980) for a provocative demographic analysis of the effect of birth cohort size on social and economic attitudes.

3.  Recent scholarship on postwar social and political change has produced a number of insightful surveys. See Chafe (1986), Hodgson (1976), and Gilbert (1986). For opposing views of the era, Diggins (1988), O'Neill (1986) and Brooks (1966) may be contrasted with Jezer (1982) and Degler (1968).

4.  A reasonable indicator of America's relative postwar wealth might be its official gold reserves; shortly after World War II, they totaled almost $25 billion, well over half the entire world's monetary gold; no other country had even $3 billion. It might also be worth noting that, buoyed by massive investment and technological innovation, much of the postwar expansion was the result of dramatic increases in productivity; for example, in 1945, manufacturing an automobile required 310 hours of labor, but by 1960 the labor hours had been halved. See U.S. Council of Economic Advisors (1986, Table B-43).

5.  Large social generalizations often leave important minorities unconsidered. Interesting historical scholarship on the postwar African-American experience includes Jaynes and Williams (1989), Farley (1984, 1987), a census monograph; and Lemann (1991). A view of black magazine publishing can be found in the autobiography of the founder of Ebony, John H. Johnson (with Lerone Bennett, Jr., 1989).

6.  For a study of changes in income and consumption for the late 1940s to the mid-1980s, see Levy (1988); see also Galbraith (1958), an influential early interpretation of postwar prosperity.

7.  Tobin is cited in Matusow (1984, p. 10). See Vatter (1963, p. 11). For similar, though less hyperbolic, celebrations of America's postwar economic performance, see Rostow (1952), Cochran (1959), and Coleman (1967).

8.  For the historical origins of the relationship between education and professional status, see Bledstein (1976). Despite its postwar expansion, however, the academy's difficulties with domestic Cold War politics is well documented in Schrecker (1986). For comparative vocational and educational data, see U.S. Department of Commerce, Bureau of the Census (1980, pp. 140, 413-488), and U.S. Department of Commerce, Bureau of the Census (1975, p. 808).

9.  For a convincing summary of the suburban American dream, see Diggins (1988, pp. 181-184). The definitive study of America's postwar residential transformation is Jackson (1985). Stilgoe (1988) and Fishman (1987) place the suburbs in a historical context. It must also

be noted that government housing policies encouraging detached, single-family home ownership played a crucial role in the postwar suburbanization process.

10. It may also be relevant, as Bourdieu's translator helpfully notes, that *jouir*, along with *jouissance*, are French slang for "sexual orgasm."

11. For historical data on leisure expenditures, see Michael (1972, pp. 33-39, 59), and U.S. Bureau of the Census (1975), pp. 316-318).

12. For a survey of American avocations, see Dulles (1965); see also Coughlin (1959, pp. 69-70, 73-74); "Recreation in the Age of Automation" (1957); and U.S. Bureau of the Census (1970, pp. 205-207).

13. For further scholarship on the domestic effects of the Cold War, see also Boyer (1985), and Wittner (1978).

14. For additional insights into the history of traditional familial practices see Caplow and Bahr (1982), a follow-up to Lynd and Lynd (1937).

15. "The Good Life," *Life* (1959, December 28, pp. 62-63). In the same issue, see also Lynes, "How Do You Rate in the New Leisure," pp. 85-89, and "Good Uses of Their Spare Time by Celebrated People," pp. 76-82.

16. See Tebbel (1969, pp. 165-180). It should also be noted that *Graham's* Magazine and *Godey's Lady's Book*, edited by Sara Josepha Hale, had substantial circulations in the 1850s, with the latter reaching a record 150,000 just before the Civil War. See Mott (1938, Vol. 1, p. 581).

17. For insights into the early influence of the *Saturday Evening Post* and *Ladies Home Journal*, see Tebbel (1948), and Bok (1920), an autobiography. Edward Bok, *The Man From Maine* (1923), is an affectionate, but readable, biography of Cyrus H.K. Curtis. See also Wood (1971a, 1971b).

18. See also McDonald (1981, pp. 50-61). For historical circulation data, see Damon-Moore (1987, pp. 19-21); see also Cohn (1987, pp. 185-215).

## CHAPTER 3

1. For an examination of the business fortunes of many of the large mass-market magazines, see also van Zuilen (1977), and Bart (1962, pp. 32-33).

2. Founded in 1924, *Liberty*, "A Weekly for Everybody," had more than 2.5 million subscribers shortly after World War II. One of its standard features was an assumed reading time (e.g., "5 Minutes 5 Seconds") posted at the beginning of each article. The magazine ceased publication in the early 1950s; see Tebbel and Zuckerman (1991, p. 193).

3. See Association of National Advertisers (1976) for historical circulation data.

4. It is important to note that, in addition to consumer magazines, trade periodicals serving professional and business markets also prospered during this time. For a solid history of the trade press, see Forsyth (1964).
5. Permission from the Ziff-Davis Publishing Company, a closely held private firm, to review company financial operating statements from this historical period is gratefully acknowledged.
6. For interesting insights into the editorial formula for the *Reader's Digest* success, see Smith and Decker-Amos (1985, pp. 127-131).
7. For an excellent review of the social impact of early American outdoors magazines, see Neuzil (1991).
8. From a management perspective, the issue of "ideational and vocabulary complexity" was an engaging one. "We always told our editors," Ziff recalled, "to write up to their audiences, which is to say that it was okay to be difficult to read if it wasn't obscurantism, that they were talking in a sophisticated way to knowledgeable people, that they didn't have to reduce things. But that always 'product' was the key. Product! Tutorial! Close analysis! The colorful writing was fun, part of the panache, but it was only window-dressing."
9. For comparison, network television's current (1992) cpm is below $5, a figure which, not coincidently, is also the cpm of *TV Guide*. Women's "service" magazines such as *Better Homes & Gardens* and *Ladies Home Journal* have cpm's below $15, and the news weeklies such as *Time* and *Newsweek* cluster around $20. Most special-interest magazines now have cpm's over $40 (Stanley R. Greenfield, chairman, Nicolas Publishing, personal interview, December 19, 1990).

## CHAPTER 4

1. For a personal narrative of some of the unrequited yearnings of the period, see Eisler (1986).
2. See also Sennett and Cobb (1972). Sklar (1975) and Biskind (1983) contain interesting insights into the film industry's cultural contradictions in the 1950s. For a thoughtful examination of the domestic tensions that may have defined the era, see Mintz and Kellogg (1988, pp. 177-201), and D'Emilio and Freedman (1988, pp. 301-325). Certainly the prevailing "Ozzie and Harriet" generality did not reflect the social reality of many women: see Davidson (1982) and Ross (1975).
3. Dickstein (1977) contains one of the more coherent and romantic formulations of this view of the 1960s. See also Zinn (1973), and for a contrasting view, Horowitz (1977).
4. For public reaction to the war, see Herring (1986, p. 173); an opposing historical interpretation can be found in Young (1991). For an

examination of the public response to the 1968 convention disorders, see Matusow (1984, pp. 423-429) and Unger and Unger (1988). Data on the communes of the 1960s can be found in "Year of the Commune," *Newsweek*, August 18, 1969, p. 89. For a thorough history of the idea of pastoralism in America, see Shi (1985).

5.  Other observers have commented on a historic American affinity for the "homely virtues of persistence, initiative, self-reliance, and independence" dating back to Benjamin Franklin's *Poor Richard's Almanac*; see Inkeles (1979, p. 398). An astute observer of the New World, Alexis de Tocqueville noted the American "habit of always considering themselves as standing alone"; see Tocqueville (1956, p. 44).

6.  For an example of the on-going academic discomfort with American's individualistic nature, see Collier (1991).

7.  See also Fasteau (1974), Brenton (1966), and Harris (1968, pp. 315-324).

8.  See also Miller (1967).

9.  Interestingly, Cancian's evidence included a study of trends in women's magazine articles. In a comparison of "traditional" themes such as self-sacrifice, shared activities, and rigid gender roles with the "modern" of self-fulfillment, individuality, privacy, and flexible gender roles, Cancian found that modern themes were represented in only 25% of the articles from 1950 and 1959, but accounted for 53% of the articles from 1960 to 1969 (Appendix II, p. 163).

10. For a scholarly critique of individualism from the opposite end of the political spectrum, see Benson and Engeman (1975). A good summary of the cultural currents of the period can be found in Clecak (1983, pp. 261-311).

11. For an earlier explication of similar sentiments, see Keniston (1965). It should be noted, however, that in a more recent study, Bellah and his colleagues have found contemporary evidence for strong cooperative and communal activity that belies some of their earlier work's conclusions; see Bellah, Madsen, Sullivan, Swidler, and Tipton (1991).

12. For an excellent rebuttal of the loss-of-community argument, see Fischer (1977, 1982); both these works document the vitality of specialized subcultures and voluntary associations.

13. One of the difficulties with Reiff's analysis centers on the question of authority's legitimacy. "The dilemma," wrote Richard Sennett, "of authority in our time, the peculiar fear it inspires, is that we feel attracted to strong figures we do not believe to be legitimate." See Sennett (1980, p. 26).

14. A possible source of difficulty for some critics of individualism might be a certain romanticism, to which Irving Kristol once offered an antidote: "Capitalism is the least romantic conception of public order that the human mind has ever conceived . . . There is no 'transcendental' dimension that is given official recognition and sanction. It

does not necessarily denigrate such things either, but, in contrast to previous societies organized around an axis of aristocratic or religious values, it relegates them to the area of individual concern, whether of the isolated individual or of voluntary associations of individuals" (1978, p. x).

15. This should not, however, be taken to mean that social station has no effect on leisure time. One study indicated that participation by members of the professional/managerial classes in active recreational pursuits such as gardening, driving for pleasure, and walking was notably higher than that of semi- or unskilled laborers; see Young and Willmott (1973, pp. 212, 216).

16. Thorstein Veblen (1934) and Josef Pieper (1963) are two of the classic analyses of leisure. For a further discussion of status issues, see Jackman and Jackman (1983), and Gilbert and Kahl (1982).

17. Cross-cultural leisure comparisons are often revealing. In the mid-1960s, less than 28% of the U.S. adult population took a vacation of six days or more, compared to an average of 44% in Europe; see Scitovsky (1976, p. 193). Additionally, European men participated in significantly more leisure activities during workdays than their American counterparts; see Ferge (1973, pp. 213-227).

18. De Grazia (1962) is a perceptive study of the relationship between work and leisure. See also Anderson (1961, 1974). Inglehart (1977) is an interesting analysis of recent value shifts.

## CHAPTER 5

1. The best quantitative comparative study of prosperity's sociocultural effects if Katona, Strumpel, and Zahn (1971).

2. See also Ball and Loy (1975), and Rader (1983).

3. See also Ewen (1988).

4. For a cross-cultural analysis of avocational interests, see Szalai (1973), and Szalai and Andrews (1980). Eisler (1983) is a popular survey of class diversions.

5. It is also interesting to contemplate the fact that some recreational equipment is encoded with social significance of a markedly different order; playing cards, for example, carry a set of popular associations far removed from notions of luxury and aristocracy.

6. For an incisive consideration of the role of education in the American class structure, see Domhoff (1978) and Silk and Silk (1980).

7. See also Smith (1963), Wolseley (1973), and Nimmo (1990, pp. 63-74).

8. For an interesting study of the postwar generational surge, see Light (1988).

9. See Compaine (1982) and Picard (1989). See also Lieberman (1977), Click and Baird (1986), Mogel (1979), and Woodress (1973).
10. For a further analysis of circulation considerations, see Bennett (1965, 1989). Additional case study material can be found in Bennack (1987) and Trowbridge (1986).
11. For circulation data, see Association of National Advertisers (1976).

## CHAPTER 6

1. See also Compaine (1974) and Television Bureau of Advertising (1959).
2. One useful way to visualize the "editorial structure" of any publications is simply to think of its Table of Contents page.
3. See also Smith (1963).
4. For a detailed analysis of the circulation of national magazines, see Swann (1975).
5. See also Picard (1989).
6. For an interesting history of the Audit Bureau of Circulations, see Bennett (1965, 1989).
7. A good overview of the departmental competition as a management strategy can be found in Wolseley (1973).
8. See also O'Toole (1985).

# BIBLIOGRAPHY

A better yesterday. (1991, October 26). *The Economist*, 1-26.

Adelson, Joseph. (1972, March 19). Is women's lib a passing fad? *New York Times Magazine*, 94.

Alpert, Hollis. (1957, 11 May). What killed Collier's? *Saturday Review*, 9-11.

America's decadent puritans. (1990, July 28). *The Economist*, 11-12.

Anderson, Nels. (1961). *Work and leisure*. New York: Free Press.

Anderson, Nels. (1974). *Man's work and leisure*. Leiden, The Netherlands: Brill

Appadurai, Arjun (Ed.). (1986). *The social life of things: Commodities in cultural perspective*. New York: Cambridge University Press.

Association of National Advertisers. (1976). *Magazine circulation and rate trends: 1940-1974*. New York: Association of National Advertisers.

Atwood, William. (1960, January 5). How America feels. *Look*, 11-15.

Bagdikian, Ben H. (1987). *The media monopoly* (2nd ed.). Boston: Beacon Press.

Ball, Donald W., & Loy, John W.(Eds.). (1975). *Sport and social order: Contributions to the sociology of sport*. Reading, MA: Addison-Wesley.

Baritz, Loren. (1990). *The good life: The meaning of success for the American middle class.* New York: Harper & Row.

Bart, Peter. (1962, Spring). Giants on uneasy footing. *Columbia Journalism Review, 1,* 32-33.

Bell, Daniel. (1960). *The end of ideology: On the exhaustion of political ideas in the fifties.* New York: Free Press.

Bell, Daniel. (1970, Fall). The cultural contradictions of capitalism. *The Public Interest, 21,* 16-43.

Bell, Daniel. (1973). *The coming of the post-industrial society: A venture in social forecasting.* New York: Basic Books.

Bell, Daniel. (1976). *The cultural contradictions of capitalism.* New York: Basic Books.

Bellah, Robert N., Madsen, Richard, Sullivan, William, Swidler, Ann, & Tipton, Steven M. (1985). *Habits of the heart: Individualism and commitment in American life.* New York: Harper & Row.

Bellah, Robert N., Madsen, Richard, Sullivan, William, Swidler, Ann, & Tipton, Steven M. (1991). *The good society.* New York: Knopf.

Bennack, Frank A. (1987). *The Hearst corporation.* New York: Newcomen Society of U.S.

Bennett, Charles O. (1965). *Facts without opinion: First fifty years of the Audit Bureau of Circulation.* Chicago: Audit Bureau of Circulation.

Bennett, Charles O. (1989). *Integrity in a changing world.* Chicago: Mobium Press.

Benson, George C.S., & Engeman, Thomas S. (1975). *Amoral America.* Stanford: Hoover Institution Press.

Biskind, Peter. (1983). *Seeing is believing: How Hollywood taught us to stop worrying and love the fifties.* New York: Pantheon.

Bledstein, Burton J. (1976). *The culture of professionalism: The middle class and the development of higher education in America.* New York: Norton.

Bogart, Leo. (1956, Spring). Magazines since the rise of television. *Journalism Quarterly, 33,* 153-166.

Bok, Edward. (1920). *The Americanization of Edward Bok.* New York: Scribner's.

Bok, Edward. (1923). *The man from Maine.* New York: Scribner's.

Bourdieu, Pierre. (1984). *Distinction: A social critique of the judgment of taste* (Richard Nice, Trans.). Cambridge: Harvard University Press.

Boyer, Paul S. (1985). *By the bomb's early light: American thought and culture at the dawn of the atomic age.* New York: Pantheon.

Brenton, Myron. (1966). *The American male.* New York: Coward-McCann.

Brooks, John. (1966). *The great leap: The past twenty-five years in America.* New York: Harper & Row.

Brown, B.W. (1982, Summer). Family intimacy in magazine advertising, 1920-1977. *Journal of Communications, 32*(3), 173-183.

Cancian, Francesca M. (1987). *Love in America: Gender and self-development.* New York: Cambridge University Press.

Caplow, Theodore, & Bahr, Howard M. (1982). *Middletown families: Fifty years of change and continuity.* Minneapolis: University of Minnesota Press.

Carey, James W. (1989). *Communication as culture: Essays on media and society.* Boston: Unwin Hyman.

Chafe, William. (1986). *The unfinished journey: America since World War II.* New York: Oxford University Press.

Charlesworth, James C. (Ed.). (1964). *Leisure in America: Blessing or curse?* Philadelphia: American Academy of Political and Social Science.

Cherlin, Andrew J. (1981). *Marriage, divorce, remarriage.* Cambridge: Harvard University Press.

Clecak, Peter. (1983). *America's quest for the ideal self: Dissent and fulfillment in the 60s and 70s.* New York: Oxford University Press.

Clecak, Peter. (1983). The movement of the 1960s and its cultural and political legacy. In S. Coben & L. Ratner (Eds.), *The development of an American culture* (pp. 261-311). New York: St. Martin's Press.

Click, J. William, & Baird, Russell N. (1986). *Magazine editing and production.* Dubuque: W.C.Brown.

Cochran, Thomas C. (1959). *Basic history of American business.* Princeton: Van Nostrand.

Cohn, Howard. (1974, November 18). Differences narrow between consumer and trade magazines. *Advertising Age,* 99-100.

Coleman, John R. (Ed.). (1967). *The changing American economy.* New York: Basic Books.

Collier, James Lincoln. (1991). *The rise of selfishness in America.* New York: Oxford University Press.

Communal living: Get together. (1991, January 26). *The Economist,* 29.

Compaine, Benjamin M. (1974). *Consumer magazines at the crossroads: A study of general and special interest magazines.* White Plains, NY: Knowledge Industry Publications.

Compaine, Benjamin M. (1980, Spring). The magazine industry: Developing the special-interest audience. *Journal of Communication,* 30(2), 98-103.

Compaine, Benjamin M. (1982). *The business of consumer magazines.* White Plains, NY: Knowledge Industry Publications.

Coughlin, Robert. (1959, December 28). A $40 billion bill just for fun. *Life,* 69-70, 73-74.

Crèvecoeur, J. Hector St. John. (1904). *Letters from an American farmer.* New York: Fox, Duffield. (Original work published 1780.)

D'Emilio, John, & Freedman, Estelle B. (1988). *Intimate matters: A history of sexuality in America.* New York: Harper & Row.

D'Emilio, John. (1983). *Sexual politics, sexual communities: The making of the homosexual minority in the United States 1940-1970.* Chicago: University of Chicago Press.

Damon-Moore, Helen Mary. (1987). *Gender and the rise of mass-circulation magazines.* (Doctoral dissertation, University of Wisconsin-Madison, 1987). Dissertation Abstracts International, 8716513.

Davenport, Walter, & Derieux, James C. (1960). *Ladies, gentlemen and editors.* Garden City, NY: Doubleday.

Davidson, Caroline. (1982). *A woman's work is never done: A history of housework in the British Isles, 1650-1950.* London: Chatto & Windus.

De Grazia, Sebastian. (1962). *Of time, work and leisure.* New York: Twentieth Century Fund.

DeFleur, Melvin. (1970). *Theories of mass communication.* New York: David McKay.

Degler, Carl N. (1968). *Affluence and anxiety, 1945-present.* Glenview, IL: Scott, Foresman.

Dickstein, Morris. (1977). *Gates of eden: American culture in the sixties.* New York: Basic Books.

Diggins, John Patrick. (1988). *The proud decades: America in war and peace, 1941-1960.* New York: Norton.

Domhoff, G. William. (1978). *The powers that be: Processes of ruling-class domination in America.* New York: Random House.

Donaldson, Scott. (1969). *The suburban myth.* New York: Columbia University Press.

Douglas, Mary, & Isherwood, Baron. (1979). *The world of goods.* New York: Basic Books.

Dulles, Foster Rhea. (1965). *A history of recreation: America learns to play* (2nd ed.). New York: Appleton-Century-Crofts.

Durkeim, Emile. (1951). *Suicide: A study in sociology* (John A. Spaulding & George Simpson, Trans.). Glencoe, IL: Free Press.

Easterlin, Richard A. (1974). Does economic growth improve the human lot? In P.A. David & M.W. Reder (Eds.), *Nations and households in economic growth: Essays in honor of Moses Abramovitz* (pp. 89-125). New York: Academic Press.

Easterlin, Richard A. (1980). *Birth and fortune: The impact of numbers on personal welfare.* New York: Basic Books.

Eisler, Benita. (1983). *Class act: America's last dirty secret.* New York: Franklin Watts.

Eisler, Benita. (1986). *Private lives: Men and women of the fifties.* New York: Franklin Watts.

Elder, Glen H. Jr. (1974). *Children of the great depression: Social change in life experience.* Chicago: University of Chicago Press.

Elson, Robert T., Prendergast, Curtis, & Colvin, Geoffrey. (1986). *The world of Time, Inc: The intimate history of a publishing enterprise, 1923-1980* (Vols. 1-3). New York: Atheneum.

Epstein, Edward Jay. (1974). *News from nowhere.* New York: Vintage Books.

Ewen, Stuart. (1976). *Captains of consciousness: Advertising and the social roots of the consumer culture.* New York: McGraw-Hill.

Ewen, Stuart. (1988). *All consuming images: The politics of style in contemporary culture.* New York: Basic Books.

Farley, Reynolds. (1984). *Blacks and whites: Narrowing the gap?* Cambridge: Harvard University Press.

Farley, Reynolds. (1987). *The color line and the quality of life in America.* New York: Russell Sage Foundation.

Fasteau, Marc Feigen. (1974). *The male machine.* New York: McGraw-Hill.

Felker, Clay. (1969, Spring). Life cycles in the age of magazines. *Antioch Review, 29, 7.*

Ferge, Susan. (1973). Social differentiation in leisure activity choices: An unfinished experiment. In A. Szalai (Ed.). *The use of time: Daily activities of urban and suburban populations in twelve countries* (pp. 213-227). The Hague, Netherlands: Mouton.

Fiedler, Leslie A. (1966). *Love and death in the American novel.* New York: Stein and Day.

Fischer, Claude S. (1977). *Networks and places: Social relations in the urban setting.* New York: Free Press.

Fischer, Claude S. (1982). *To dwell among friends: Personal networks in town and city.* Chicago: University of Chicago Press.

Fishman, Robert. (1987). *Bourgeois utopias: The rise and fall of suburbia.* New York: Basic Books.

Fletcher, Alan D. (1977). City magazines find a niche in the media marketplace. *Journalism Quarterly, 54*(4), 740-743.

Fletcher, Alan D., & Winn, Paul D. (1974, Autumn). An intermagazine analysis of factors in advertising readership. *Journalism Quarterly, 51*(3), 425-430.

Ford, James L.C. (1969). *Magazines for millions.* Carbondale: Southern Illinois University Press.

Forsyth, David P. (1964). *The business press in America, 1750-1865.* Philadelphia: Chilton Books.

Friedrich, Otto. (1970). *Decline and fall.* New York: Harper & Row.

Galbraith, John Kenneth. (1958). *The affluent society.* Boston: Houghton Mifflin.

Galbraith, John Kenneth. (1967). *The new industrial state.* Boston: Houghton Mifflin.

Gallup, George. (1960, October 2). *Gallup organization survey.* (Dialog file 468, items 00037162-00037163).

Gans, Herbert J. (1967). *The Levittowners: Ways of life and politics in a new suburban community.* New York: Knopf.

Gans, Herbert J. (1975). *Popular culture and high culture: An analysis and evaluation of taste.* New York: Basic Books.

Gans, Herbert J. (1988). *Middle American individualism: The future of liberal democracy.* New York: Free Press.

Gerlach, P. (1987, Spring). Research about magazines appearing in Journalism Quarterly. *Journalism Quarterly, 64*(1), 178-182.

Gilbert, Dennis, & Kahl, Joseph A. (1982). *The American class structure: A new synthesis.* Homewood, IL: Dorsey Press.

Gilbert, James. (1986). *Another chance: Postwar America, 1945-1985* (2nd ed.). Chicago: Dorsey Press.

Gilligan, Carol. (1982). *In a different voice: Psychological theory and women's development.* Cambridge: Harvard University Press.

The good life. (1959, December 28). *Life,* 62-63.
Good uses of their spare time by celebrated people. (1959, December 28). *Life,* 76-82.
Gordon, George N. (1975). *Communications and media.* New York: Hastings House.
Gordon, George N. (1977). *The communications revolution.* New York: Hastings House.
Greene, Theodore. (1970). *America's heroes: The changing models of success in American magazines.* New York: Oxford University Press.
Hague, John A. (Ed.). (1964). *American character and culture: Some twentieth century perspectives.* Deland, FL: Everett Edwards Press.
Harris, T. George. (1968). From rugged-individualism to helpless-individualism. In J.G. Kirk (Ed.). *America now.* New York: Atheneum.
Hartshorne, Thomas L. (1968). *The distorted image: Changing conceptions of the American character since Turner.* Cleveland: Case Western Reserve University Press.
Herring, George C. (1986). *America's longest war: The United States and Vietnam, 1950-1975* (2nd ed.). New York: Knopf.
Hirsch, Fred. (1976). *Social limits to growth.* Cambridge: Harvard University Press.
Hodgson, Godfrey. (1976). *America in our time: From World War II to Nixon, what happened and why.* New York: Vintage Books.
Holder, Stephen. (1972). The death of the Saturday Evening Post, 1960-1970: A popular culture phenomenon. In R.B. Nye (Ed.), *New dimensions in popular culture* (pp. 78-89). Bowling Green, OH: Bowling Green University Popular Press.
Horowitz, Irving Louis. (1977). *Ideology and utopia in the United States, 1956-1976.* New York: Oxford University Press.
Inglehart, Ronald. (1977). *The silent revolution: Changing values and political styles among western publics.* Princeton: Princeton University Press.
Inkeles, Alex. (1979). Continuity and change in the American national character. In S.M. Lipset (Ed.), *The third century: America as a post-industrial society* (pp. 389-416). Stanford: Hoover Institution Press, Stanford University.
Innis, Harold A. (1950). *Empire and communications.* Toronto: University of Toronto Press.
Innis, Harold A. (1951). *The bias of communication.* Toronto: University of Toronto Press.
Jackman, Mary R., & Jackman, Robert W. (1983). *Class awareness in the United States.* Berkeley: University of California Press.
Jackson, Kenneth T. (1985). *The crabgrass frontier: The suburbanization of the United States.* New York: Oxford University Press.
Jacobson, J. (1988, Summer). Research activity of magazine publishing. *Journalism Quarterly, 65*(2), 511-514.
Jacoby, J., & Hoyer, W.D. (1987). *The comprehension and miscomprehension of print communications: An investigation of mass media magazines.* Hillsdale, NJ: Erlbaum.

Janello, Amy, & Jones, Brennon. (1991). *The American magazine.* New York: Harry Abrams.

Jaynes, Gerald David, & Williams, Robin M. Jr. (Eds.). (1989). *A common destiny: Black and American society.* Washington, DC: National Academy Press.

Jezer, Marty. (1982). *The dark ages: Life in the United States, 1945-1960.* Boston: South End Press.

Johnson, John H. (with Bennett, Lerone Jr). (1989). *Succeeding against the odds.* New York: Warner Books.

Jones, Landon Y. (1980). *Great expectations: America and the baby boom generation.* New York: Ballantine Books.

Katona, George, Strumpel, Burkhard, & Zahn, Ernest. (1971). *Aspirations and affluence: Comparative studies in the United States and western Europe.* New York, McGraw-Hill.

Kaul, Arthur J., & McKerns, Joseph P. (1985, August). *Long waves and journalism ideology in America, 1835-1985.* Paper presented at the annual meeting of the Association of Education in Journalism and Mass Communication, Memphis, TN.

Keniston, Kenneth. (1965). *The uncommitted: Alienated youth in American society.* New York: Harcourt Brace.

Kinnear, T.C., Horne, D.A., & Zingery, T.A. (1986). Valid magazine audience measurement: Issues and perspective. In J.H. Leigh & C.R. Martin, Jr. (Eds.), *Current issues and research in advertising 1986* (pp 261-270). Ann Arbor: University of Michigan Graduate School of Business.

Koback, James B. (1972, September/October). The life cycle of a magazine. *Folio, 1,* 45.

Kobler, John. (1968). *Luce: His time, life and fortune.* Garden City, NY: Doubleday.

Krishnan, R., & Soley, L.C. (1987, August/September). Controlling magazine circulation. *Journal of Advertising Research, 27*(4 ), 17-23.

Lancaster, Kelvin. (1966). A new approach to consumer theory. *Journal of Political Economy, 74,* 132-157.

Lasch, Christopher. (1977). *Haven in a heartless world: The family besieged.* New York: Basic Books.

Lasch, Christopher. (1978). *The culture of narcissism: American life in the age of diminishing expectations.* New York: Norton.

Lasswell, Harold D. (1972). The structure and function of communication on society. In W. Schramm (Ed.), *Mass communications* (pp. 117-130). Urbana: University of Illinois Press.

Lears, Jackson. (1989). A matter of taste: Corporate cultural hegemony in a mass-consumption society. In L. May (Ed.), *Recasting America* (pp. 38-57). Chicago: University of Chicago Press.

Lemann, Nicholas. (1991). *The promised land: The great black migration and how it changed America.* New York: Knopf.

Levy, Frank. (1988). *Dollars and dreams: The changing American income distribution.* New York: Norton.

Lieberman, Seymour. (1977). *How and why people buy magazines.* Port Washington: Publishers Clearing House.

Light, Paul C. (1989) *Baby boomers.* New York: Norton.

Linder, Staffan B. (1970). *The harried leisure class.* New York: Columbia University Press.

Lynd, Robert Staughton, & Lynd, Helen Merrell. (1937). *Middletown in transition: A study in cultural conflicts.* New York: Harcourt Brace.

Lynes, Russell. (1959, December 28). How do you rate in the new leisure. *Life,* 85-89.

Mailer, Norman. (1954, Autumn). David Reisman reconsidered. *Dissent,* 358-359.

Maisel, S. Richard. (1973, Summer). The decline of mass media. *The Public Opinion Quarterly, 37,* 159-170.

Marx, Karl. (1964). *Economic and philosophical manuscripts of 1844.* (Dirk J. Struik, Ed., Martin Milligan Trans.). New York: International Publishers.

Matusow, Allen J. (1984). *The unraveling of America.* New York: Harper & Row.

McDonald, S.W. (1981, Fall). Two popular editors of the gilded age: Mass culture, magazines, and correspondence. *Journal of Popular Culture, 15*(20), 50-61.

McEvoy, George F., & Vincent, Cynthia S. (1980, Winter). Who reads and why? *Journal of Communication, 30*(1), 134-140.

McFadden, Maureen. (1983, July). Why some magazines are replacing fiction with fact. *Magazine Age,* 22-26.

Menon, Anil, Bush, Alan J., & Smart, Denise T. (1987, October-November). Media habits of the do-it-yourselfers. *Journal of Advertising Research, 27*(5), 14-20.

Merrill, John C., & Lowenstein, Ralph L. (1979). *Media, messages and men: New perspectives in communication* (2nd ed.). New York: Longman.

Michael, Robert T. (1972). *The effect of education on efficiency in consumption.* New York: National Bureau of Economic Research.

Miller, David L. (1967). *Individualism: Personal achievement and the open society.* Austin: University of Texas Press.

Mintz, Steven, & Kellogg, Susan. (1988). *Domestic revolutions: A social history of American family life.* New York: Free Press.

Mogel, Leonard. (1979). *The magazine.* Englewood Cliffs, NJ: Prentice-Hall.

Mooney, Michael. (1969, November). The death of the Saturday Evening Post. *The Atlantic Monthly,* 73-75.

Mott, Frank Luther. (1938). *A history of American magazines* (Vols. 1-5). Cambridge: Harvard University Press.

Neuzil, Mark. (1991, April). *Sporting journals, power groups and culture in 19th century America: The case of forest and stream and hunting ethics.* Paper presented at the midyear meeting of the Magazine Division of the Association of Education in Journalism and Mass Communication, Williamsburg, VA.

Nimmo, Dan. (1990). Popular magazines, popular communication, and politics. In R.L. Savage & D. Nimmo (Eds.), *Politics in familiar contexts: Projecting politics through popular media* (pp. 63-74). Norwood, NJ: Ablex.

Nord, David Paul. (1980, Spring). An economic perspective on formula in popular culture. *Journal of American Culture, 3,* 17-31.

Nye, Russel B. (1970). *The unembarrassed muse: The popular arts in America.* New York: Dial Press.

O'Neill, William L. (1986). *American high: The years of confidence, 1945-1960.* New York: Free Press.

O'Toole, John E. (1985). *The trouble with advertising: A view from the inside* (2nd ed.). New York: Times Books.

The open society and its enemies revisited. (1988, April 23). *The Economist,* 19-22.

Parsons, Talcott. (1966). *Societies: Evolutionary and comparative perspectives.* Englewood Cliffs, NJ: Prentice-Hall.

Pauly, John J. (1991, February). A beginner's guide to qualitative research in mass communications. *Journalism Monographs, 125.*

Peterson, Theodore. (1956). *Magazines in the twentieth century.* Urbana: University of Illinois Press.

Picard, Robert G. (1989). *Media economics: Concepts and issues.* Newbury Park, CA: Sage.

Pieper, Josef. (1963). *Leisure, the basis of culture* (Rev. ed.). (Alexander Dru, Trans.). New York: Pantheon.

Pirsig, Robert. (1974). *Zen and the art of motorcycle maintenance: An inquiry into values.* New York: Morrow.

Postman, Neil. (1985). *Amusing ourselves to death: Public discourse in the age of show business.* New York: Viking.

Postman, Neil. (1988). *Conscientious objections: Stirring up trouble about language, technology and education.* New York: Knopf.

Puliyel, T. (1986, April). High readers-per-copy: An attempt at validation. *Journal of the Market Research Society, 28*(2), 115-124.

Rader, Benjamin G. (1983). *American sports: From the age of folk games to the age of spectators.* Englewood Cliffs, NJ: Prentice-Hall.

Rankin, William Parkman. (1984). *The evolution of the business management of selected general consumer magazines.* New York: Praeger.

Recreation in the age of automation. (1957, September). *Annals of the American Academy of Political and Social Sciences, 313.*

Richardson, Lyon N. (1931). *A history of early American magazines, 1741-1789.* New York: Nelson and Sons.

Rieff, Philip. (1966). *The triumph of the therapeutic: Uses of faith after Freud.* New York: Harper & Row.

Riesman, David. (1950). *The lonely crowd: A study of the changing American character.* New Haven: Yale University Press.

Riesman, David. (1958). The suburban sadness. In W.M. Dobriner (Ed.), *The suburban community* (pp. 375-408). New York: Putnam.

Riesman, David. (1964). *Abundance for what? and other essays.* Garden City, NY: Doubleday.

Robinson, John P. (1980, Winter). The changing reading habits of the American public. *Journal of Communication, 30*(1), 141-152.

Ross, Heather L. (1975). *Time of transition: The growth of families headed by women.* Washington, DC: Urban Institute.

Rostow, Walt W. (1952). *The process of economic growth.* New York: Norton.

Schickel, Robert. (1990, October). Homebodies. *Memories,* 18-19.

Schmidt, Dorothy S. (Ed.). (1979). *The American magazine, 1890-1940.* Wilmington: Delaware Art Museum.

Schmidt, Dorothy S. (Ed.). (1980). Focus on magazines. *Journal of American Culture, 3,* 1-2.

Schmidt, Dorothy S. (1980, Spring). Magazines, technology, and American culture. *Journal of American Culture, 3,* 3-16.

Schmidt, Dorothy, S. (1989). Magazines. In M.T. Ingre (Ed.), *Handbook of American popular culture* (2nd ed., pp. 641-669). Westport, CT: Greenwood Press.

Schrecker, Ellen W. (1986). *No ivory tower: McCarthyism and the universities.* New York: Oxford University Press.

Scitovsky, Tibor. (1976). *The joyless economy: An inquiry into human satisfaction and consumer dissatisfaction.* New York: Oxford University Press.

Sennett, Richard. (1977). *The fall of public man.* New York: Knopf.

Sennett, Richard. (1980). *Authority.* New York: Knopf.

Sennett, Richard, & Cobb, Jonathan. (1972). *The hidden injuries of class.* New York: Vintage.

Servan-Schreiber, Jean-Louis. (1978). *The power to inform.* New York: McGraw-Hill.

Shi, David. (1985). *The simple life: Plain living and high thinking in American culture.* New York: Oxford University Press.

Silk, Leonard, & Silk, Mark. (1980). *The American establishment.* New York: Basic Books.

Simmel, Georg. (1978). *The philosophy of money.* (Tom Bottomore & David Frisby, Trans.). Boston: Routledge & Kegan Paul.

Sklar, Robert. (1975). *Movie-made America: A cultural history of American movies.* New York: Random House.

Smigel, Erwin O. (Ed.). (1963). *Work and leisure: A contemporary social problem.* New Haven, CT: College and University Press.

Smith, R.F., & Decker-Amos, L. (1985, Spring). Of lasting interest? A study of change in the content of the *Reader's Digest. Journalism Quarterly, 62*(1), 127-131.

Smith, Roger H. (Ed.). (1963). *The American reading public: What it reads, why it reads.* New York: R.R. Bowker.

Soley, L.C., & Krishnan, R. (1987). Does advertising subsidize consumer magazine prices? *Journal of Advertising, 16*(2), 4-9.

Spencer, Steven. (1966, January 16). The birth control revolution. *Saturday Evening Post*, 22.

Spindler, George D. (1977). Change and continuity in American core values: An anthropological perspective. In G. Di Renzo (Ed.), *We the people: American character and social change* (pp. 20-39). Westport, CT: Greenwood Press.

Stearns, Peter N. (1990). *Be a man! Males in modern society*. New York: Holmes & Meier.

Stilgoe, John R. (1988). *Borderland: Origins of the American suburb, 1820-1939*. New Haven, CT: Yale University Press.

Strumpel, Burkhard (Ed.). (1974). *Subjective elements of well-being: Papers presented at a seminar of the organisation for economic co-operation and development*. Paris: Organisation for Economic Co-operation and Development.

Strumpel, Burkhard (Ed.). (1976). *Economic means for human needs: Social indicators of well-being and discontent*. Ann Arbor: Survey Research Center, Institute for Social Research, University of Michigan.

Susman, Warren. (1989). Did success spoil the United States? Dual representations in postwar America. In L. May (Ed.), *Recasting America* (pp. 19-37). Chicago: University of Chicago Press.

Swados, Harvey. (1958). Less work—less leisure. In E. Larrabee & R. Meyersohn (Eds.), *Mass leisure* (pp. 353-363). Glencoe, IL: Free Press.

Swann, Michael M. (1975). *Mass magazine circulation patterns in the United States*. Syracuse, NY: Geography Discussion Paper Series.

Szalai, Alexander (Ed.). (1973). *The use of time: Daily activities of urban and suburban populations in twelve countries*. The Hague, Netherlands: Mouton.

Szalai, Alexander, & Andrews, Frank M. (Eds.). (1980). *The quality of life: Comparative studies*. Beverly Hills, CA: Sage.

Taft, William H. (1982). *American magazines for the 1980s*. New York: Hastings House.

Tebbel, John W. (1948). *George Horace Lorimer and The Saturday Evening Post*. Garden City, NY: Doubleday.

Tebbel, John W. (1969). *The American magazine: A compact history*. New York: Hawthorn.

Tebbel, John W., & Zuckerman, Mary Ellen. (1991). *The magazine in America, 1741-1990*. New York: Oxford University Press.

Television Bureau of Advertising. (1959). *The changing face of magazines*. New York: Author.

Tiger, Lionel. (1969). *Men in groups*. New York: Random House.

Tocqueville, Alexis de. (1956). *Democracy in America*. (Richard D. Heffner, Ed. & Abr.). New York: New American Library. (Original work published in 1835)

Tönnies, Ferdinand. (1940). *Fundamental concepts of sociology* (Gemeinschaft und Gesellschaft). (Charles P. Loomis, Trans.). New York: American Book.

Trowbridge, C. Robertson. (1986). *Yankee Publishing, Inc.: Fifty years of preserving New England's culture while extending its influence.* New York: Newcomen Society of U.S.

U.S. Council of Economic Advisors. (1986). *Economic report of the President: 1986.* Washington, DC: U.S. Government Printing Office.

U.S. Department of Commerce, Bureau of the Census. (1950-1980). *Statistical Abstract of the United States.* Washington, DC: U.S. Government Printing Office.

U.S. Department of Commerce, Bureau of the Census. (1975). *Historical statistics of the United States: Colonial times to 1970.* Washington, DC: U.S. Government Printing Office.

U.S. Department of Commerce, Bureau of the Census. (1977). *Census of manufacturers.* Washington, DC: U.S. Government Printing Office.

U.S. Department of Commerce, Bureau of Economic Analysis. (1965, 1971, 1976). *U.S. industrial outlook.* Washington, DC: U.S. Government Printing Office.

Unger, Irwin, & Unger, Debi. (1988). *Turning point, 1968.* New York: Scribner.

Van Zuilen, Antoon J. (1977). *The life cycle of magazines: A historical study of the decline and fall of the general interest mass audience magazine in the United States during the period 1946-1972.* Uithoorn, Netherlands: Graduate Press.

Vatter, Harold G. (1963). *The U.S. economy in the 1950s: An economic history.* New York: Norton.

Veblen, Thorstein. (1934). *The theory of the leisure class: An economic study of institutions.* New York: Modern Library.

Veroff, Joseph, Douran, Elizabeth, & Kulka, Richard. (1981). *The inner American: A self-portrait from 1957 to 1976.* New York: Basic Books.

Victory Celebrations. (1945, August 27). *Life,* 21-27.

White, Theodore H. (1968). *The view from the fortieth floor.* New York: Avon.

Whyte, William H. (1956). *The organization man.* New York: Simon & Schuster.

Wittner, Lawrence S. (1978). *Cold war America: From Hiroshima to Watergate.* New York: Holt, Rinehart & Winston.

Wolfe, Tom. (1976, August 30). The 'me' decade and the third great awakening. *New West,* 25-32.

Wolfenstein, Martha. (1958). The emergence of fun morality. In E. Larrabee & R. Meyersohn (Eds.), *Mass leisure* (pp. 86-97). Glencoe, IL: Free Press.

Wolseley, Roland E. (1951). *The magazine world: An introduction to magazine journalism.* New York: Prentice-Hall.

Wolseley, Roland E. (1973). *The changing magazine: Trends in readership and management.* New York: Hastings House.

Wolseley, Ronald E. (1977). The role of magazines in the U.S.A. *Gazette, 23*(1), 20-26.

Wood, James Playsted. (1971a). *Magazines in the United States.* New York: Roland Press.

Wood, James Playsted. (1971b). *The Curtis magazines.* New York: Roland Press.

Wood, Robert C. (1958). *Suburbia: Its people and their politics.* Boston: Houghton Mifflin.

Woodress, James (Ed.). (1973). *Essays mostly on periodical publishing in America.* Durham, NC: Duke University Press.

Yankelovich, Daniel. (1974). *The new morality: A profile of American youth in the seventies.* New York: McGraw-Hill.

Yankelovich, Daniel. (1981). *New rules: Searching for fulfillment in a world turned upside down.* New York: Random House.

Year of the commune. (1969, August 18). *Newsweek,* 89.

Young, Marilyn. (1991). *The Vietnam wars, 1945-1990.* New York: HarperCollins.

Young, Michael, & Willmott, Peter. (1973) *The symmetrical family.* New York: Pantheon.

Zaretsky, Eli. (1976). *Capitalism, the family and personal life.* New York: Harper & Row.

Zinn, Howard. (1973). *Postwar America: 1945-1971.* Indianapolis: Bobbs-Merrill.

# Author Index

# SUBJECT INDEX